FOUNDATIONS OF THE CHRISTIAN RELIGION

FOUNDATIONS OF THE CHRISTIAN RELIGION

Blaise Pascal

Translated by W. F. Trotter

RELEVANT BOOKS

Published by RELEVANT Books
A division of RELEVANT Media Group, Inc.

www.relevantbooks.com
www.relevantmediagroup.com

© 2006 RELEVANT Media Group

Design by RELEVANT Solutions
Cover design by Ben Pieratt
Interior design by Ben Pieratt, Jeremy Kennedy, Anna Melcon, Aaron Maurer

Pensées is in the public domain. Text taken from www.ccel.org.

For information or bulk orders:
RELEVANT MEDIA GROUP, INC.
100 SOUTH LAKE DESTINY DR., STE 200
ORLANDO, FL 32810
407-660-1411

Library of Congress Control Number: 2005911204
International Standard Book Number: 0-9776167-7-0

06 07 08 09 10 8 7 6 5 4 3 2 1

Printed in the United States of America

This book excerpts Sections II, IV, V, and VIII
from Blaise Pascal's *Pensées*.

CONTENTS

INTRODUCTION

I came upon the works of Blaise Pascal as a college student in a critical time of my faith development. Having grown up in a baby-boomer, evangelical home, Christianity was as common to me as apple pie and America. But my college studies—even at a Christian college—had exposed me to a much wider, more intellectual world. I found myself grappling with the philosophers' existential questions of basic existence, the sociological and psychological explanations of what I had always thought were strictly spiritual influences, and the discovery that the students' anti-war, civil rights movement was striking a chord inside my heart and mind that was suddenly causing me to question not only the political system, but all authoritative organizations, including what we called the "institutional Church." Throwing my own personal faith into the mix was just another step in the deconstruction. I always thought the early reality of my experience with Christ was impervious to doubt, but I had to be honest and add my faith to the intellectual quest, even if my heart was convinced of the answer.

During this time, three writers greatly influenced my

faith-reconstruction process: C.S. Lewis, for his careful apologetics; Francis Schaeffer, for his integration of philosophy and biblical theology; and the seventeenth-century mathematician, physicist, and religious thinker Blaise Pascal, for his passion for the truth and his methodical approach to understanding it. Pascal is especially thrilling because despite the span of years and cultures that separates us, the ringing relevancy of his arguments still connects today.

I have a great admiration for Christians who have excelled at things other than being Christian. And when someone with worldly knowledge speaks about religion, and speaks well, it brings a greater credibility to his argument. Pascal was such a figure.

It is almost as if, in his short life of thirty-nine years, Pascal lived two lives and stood out in them both. His first, starting from his teenage years and continuing until he was thirty, was as a mathematical genius and physicist known for his early experiments on air pressure and the existence of a vacuum. From mathematical theorems still in use today to computer software bearing his name, Pascal is a household word in science. This was also a time he vacillated between the worldly and fashionable life of Paris and the rigorous religious pursuit that had captured his sister and his father late in his life.

But at the age of thirty-one, confused and unhappy, Pascal began to seek God intensely through the Scriptures. On the night of November 23, 1654, while reading the seventeenth chapter of the Gospel of John, Pascal had an encounter with God that instantly filled the emptiness in his heart. It was a life-changing experience he would memorialize on a parchment he had sewn into the lining of his coat until his death eight years later.

On that night, he wrote:

> From about half past ten at night to about half an hour after midnight,
> FIRE
> "God of Abraham, God of Isaac, God of Jacob," not of philosophers and scholars
> Certitude, heartfelt joy, peace.
> God of Jesus Christ.
> God of Jesus Christ.
> The world forgotten, everything except God.
> He can only be found by the ways that have been taught in the Gospels.
> Greatness of the human soul.
> "O righteous Father, the world has not known You, but I have known You" (John 17:25).
> Joy, joy, joy, tears of joy.

This was the synthesis Pascal was looking for. His brilliant mind had taken him so far in his quest for truth, but knowledge alone could not satisfy. In many ways he was a seventeenth-century Solomon who knew that man is caught in a dialectical tension. His intellect gave him nobility, but his search for happiness was forever frustrated. Pascal's catalyst came through the realization that faith sees beyond the limits of reason. "The heart has its reasons, that reason knows not of."

The result was a passion in his writing and apologetic for the Christian faith that many consider to be the pinnacle of French prose. His scientific brilliance was matched by his literary excellence, so that he is now known as much for his work in literature as he is for his work in science. I doubt there is a literary or law degree in the Western world that does not include, as its foundational study, the writings and argumentative skills of Pascal.

Now his writing burned with the fire of his love for God, the truth of the Scriptures, and an understanding of the limits of reason. He still employed his brilliant intellect, only now he used it to explain what we can't know through intellect alone. Works such as "Reason Can Begin Again by Recognizing What It Can Never Know" and "The Transition from Human Knowledge to Knowing God" are indications of his new message to other intellectuals. It is not sufficient to know about

God or even argue His existence (which Pascal could do better than anybody); ultimately, it was necessary to meet God and come to know Him personally.

I will never travel as far down the intellectual road as Pascal did—I have neither the IQ nor the patience—but the fact that he did, and came back to tell us that road ultimately leads to a dead end, is enough for me to go back to my experience of Christ and line my pockets with its preciousness as dearly as he did. It's also enough to show me what my intellect is for. Intellect finally tells us what we need to know—that it cannot deliver everything. *Well, then*, you might think, *why bother?* Why not just take Pascal's word for it and go on your way? Why do you have to plod down this road at all? Because your mind is your own, and you must find out as much as you can for yourself. Otherwise, you will not be able to love God fully. Like me, you will probably not travel as far down this road as Pascal did, but you need to travel far enough so that when you meet him coming back, you will have learned enough yourself to know what he is talking about.

Three hundred and fifty years ago, one of the greatest minds in human history trembled in the presence of God and cried tears of joy over his salvation. Now, scholars, scientists, and lawyers have to read about it, because he wrote it so well. That alone is a testimony for others to follow.

I make no illusions about how to read Pascal; it will be difficult. I can almost guarantee you will be tempted to give up. For a sound-bite generation to follow someone measuring out each thought is an education in itself. But the rewards are great.

The key will be to keep moving forward. As Francis Schaeffer used to teach, "Keep on keeping on!" You will find names and cultural issues you know nothing of. These writings were in part a public discourse with other intellectuals and religious figures of the time. And you will find that thoughts will be unconnected. Much of the *Pensées* are taken from his notes, as from a notebook, recording what he thought when he thought it. Though the selected sections follow a cohesive pattern, the inner writings may not. For this reason, it's not imperative to read from beginning to end. It's a little like the wisdom literature of the Bible (Proverbs, Ecclesiastes); you can pretty much pick it up anywhere and find something relevant to life and faith. You can ignore the numbering system (necessary in the translation), although longer, unnumbered sections do indicate more development on a particular theme.

Pascal is a little like a roller coaster: you hang on for the ride. Sometimes it will seem as if you are hardly moving, and then you will crest on a thought and resonate with the exhilarating downhill slope of discovery. My encouragement is to keep reading. You will have to use your mind as you perhaps never have before, and even then you may have to pass through parts you don't understand.

Perhaps Pascal himself offers the best advice: "When we read too fast or too slowly, we understand nothing."

John Fischer
Senior writer for PurposeDrivenLife.com
Author of *Confessions of a Caffeinated Christian*

BIOGRAPHY OF BLAISE PASCAL

Full Name: Blaise Pascal

Date of Birth: June 19, 1623 CE

Family Stats: The third of Étienne Pascal's children and his only son. His mother, Antoinette Begon, died when he was only three years old.

Lived In: Born in Clermont, in the Auvergne region of France; later lived in Paris, Rouen, and Port Royal.

Occupation: Mathematician, physicist, and religious philosopher

Claim to Fame: Pascal's earliest work was in the natural and applied sciences, where he made advancements in the construction of mechanical calculators and the study of fluids, and clarified the concepts of pressure and vacuum. Pascal also wrote powerfully in defense of the scientific method and, with Fermat, laid the foundation for the theory of probability.

In literature, Pascal is regarded as one of the most important authors of the French Classical Period, and today is considered one of the greatest masters of French prose. He is best known for his collection of spiritual essays, *Pensées*.

Famous Quote: "If God does not exist, one will lose nothing by believing in him, while if he does exist, one will lose everything by not believing."

Famous Works: *Pensées, Lettres Provinciales*

Died: August 19, 1662, in Paris, France, from a brain hemorrhage due to a malignant growth in his stomach that had spread to the brain. He was thirty-nine.

Conversion Experience: After his father injured his leg in 1646, he was looked after by two brothers from a nearby religious movement. They had a profound effect on the young Pascal, and he became deeply religious. Sometime around October 1654 he was involved in a near-fatal accident. The horses pulling his carriage bolted, leaving the carriage hanging over a bridge above the Seine River. Although he suffered no physical injury, it appears that he was much affected psychologically. Not long after, on November 23, 1654, he underwent another religious experience and pledged his life to Christianity.

Miscellaneous Fact: His last words were "May God never abandon me."

SECTION II.

The Misery of Man Without God

60. First part: Misery of man without God.

Second part: Happiness of man with God.

Or, First part: That nature is corrupt. Proved by nature itself.

Second part: That there is a Redeemer. Proved by Scripture.

61. Order.—I might well have taken this discourse in an order like this: to show the vanity of all conditions of men, to show the vanity of ordinary lives, and then the vanity of philosophic lives, sceptics, stoics; but the order would not have been kept. I know a little what it is, and how few people understand it. No human science can keep it. Saint Thomas did not keep it. Mathematics keep it, but they are useless on account of their depth.

62. Preface to the first part.—To speak of those who have treated of the knowledge of self; of the divisions of

Charron, which sadden and weary us; of the confusion of Montaigne; that he was quite aware of his want of method and shunned it by jumping from subject to subject; that he sought to be fashionable.

His foolish project of describing himself! And this not casually and against his maxims, since every one makes mistakes, but by his maxims themselves, and by first and chief design. For to say silly things by chance and weakness is a common misfortune, but to say them intentionally is intolerable, and to say such as that...

63. Montaigne.—Montaigne's faults are great. Lewd words; this is bad, notwithstanding Mademoiselle de Gournay. Credulous; people without eyes. Ignorant; squaring the circle, a greater world. His opinions on suicide, on death. He suggests an indifference about salvation, without fear and without repentance. As his book was not written with a religious purpose, he was not bound to mention religion; but it is always our duty not to turn men from it. One can excuse his rather free and licentious opinions on some relations of life; but one cannot excuse his thoroughly pagan views on death, for a man must renounce piety altogether, if he does not at least wish to die like a Christian. Now, through the whole of his book his only conception of death is a cowardly and effeminate one.

64. It is not in Montaigne, but in myself, that I find all that I see in him.

65. What good there is in Montaigne can only have been acquired with difficulty. The evil that is in him, I mean apart from his morality, could have been corrected in a moment, if he had been informed that he made too much of trifles and spoke too much of himself.

66. One must know oneself. If this does not serve to discover truth, it at least serves as a rule of life, and there is nothing better.

67. The vanity of the sciences.—Physical science will not console me for the ignorance of morality in the time of affliction. But the science of ethics will always console me for the ignorance of the physical sciences.

68. Men are never taught to be gentlemen and are taught everything else; and they never plume themselves so much on the rest of their knowledge as on knowing how to be gentlemen. They only plume themselves on knowing the one thing they do not know.

69. The infinites, the mean.—When we read too fast or too slowly, we understand nothing.

70. Nature...—Nature has set us so well in the centre,

that if we change one side of the balance, we change the other also. This makes me believe that the springs in our brain are so adjusted that he who touches one touches also its contrary.

71. Too much and too little wine. Give him none, he cannot find truth; give him too much, the same.

72. Man's disproportion.—This is where our innate knowledge leads us. If it be not true, there is no truth in man; and if it be true, he finds therein great cause for humiliation, being compelled to abase himself in one way or another. And since he cannot exist without this knowledge, I wish that, before entering on deeper researches into nature, he would consider her both seriously and at leisure, that he would reflect upon himself also, and knowing what proportion there is... Let man then contemplate the whole of nature in her full and grand majesty, and turn his vision from the low objects which surround him. Let him gaze on that brilliant light, set like an eternal lamp to illumine the universe; let the earth appear to him a point in comparison with the vast circle described by the sun; and let him wonder at the fact that this vast circle is itself but a very fine point in comparison with that described by the stars in their revolution round the firmament. But if our view be arrested there, let our imagination pass beyond; it will sooner exhaust the power of conception than

nature that of supplying material for conception. The whole visible world is only an imperceptible atom in the ample bosom of nature. No idea approaches it. We may enlarge our conceptions beyond an imaginable space; we only produce atoms in comparison with the reality of things. It is an infinite sphere, the centre of which is everywhere, the circumference nowhere. In short, it is the greatest sensible mark of the almighty power of God that imagination loses itself in that thought.

Returning to himself, let man consider what he is in comparison with all existence; let him regard himself as lost in this remote corner of nature; and from the little cell in which he finds himself lodged, I mean the universe, let him estimate at their true value the earth, kingdoms, cities, and himself. What is a man in the Infinite?

But to show him another prodigy equally astonishing, let him examine the most delicate things he knows. Let a mite be given him, with its minute body and parts incomparably more minute, limbs with their joints, veins in the limbs, blood in the veins, humours in the blood, drops in the humours, vapours in the drops. Dividing these last things again, let him exhaust his powers of conception, and let the last object at which he can arrive be now that of our discourse. Perhaps he will think that here is the smallest point in nature. I will let him see therein a new abyss. I will paint for him not only the visible universe, but all that he can conceive of nature's immensity in the womb of this abridged atom. Let him see therein an infinity of universes, each of which has its firmament, its planets, its earth, in the same proportion as in the visible world; in each earth animals, and in the last mites, in which he will find again all that the first had, finding still in these others the same thing without end and without cessation. Let him lose himself in wonders as amazing in their littleness as the others in their vastness. For who will not be astounded at the fact that our body, which a little while ago was imperceptible in the universe, itself imperceptible in the bosom of the whole, is now a colossus, a world, or rather a whole, in respect of the nothingness which we cannot reach? He who regards himself in this light will be afraid of himself, and observing himself sustained in the body given him by nature between those two abysses of the Infinite and Nothing, will tremble at the sight of these marvels; and I think that, as his curiosity changes into admiration, he will be more disposed to contemplate them in silence than to examine them with presumption.

For, in fact, what is man in nature? A Nothing in comparison with the Infinite, an All in comparison with the Nothing, a mean between nothing and everything. Since he is infinitely removed from comprehending the extremes, the end of things and their beginning are hopelessly hidden from him in an impenetrable secret; he is equally incapable of seeing the Nothing from which he was made, and the Infinite in which he is swallowed up.

What will he do then, but perceive the appearance of the middle of things, in an eternal despair of knowing either their beginning or their end. All things proceed from the Nothing, and are borne towards the Infinite. Who will follow these marvellous processes? The Author of these wonders understands them. None other can do so.

Through failure to contemplate these Infinites, men have rashly rushed into the examination of nature, as though they bore some proportion to her. It is strange that they have wished to understand the beginnings of things, and thence to arrive at the knowledge of the whole, with a presumption as infinite as their object. For surely this design cannot be formed without presumption or without a capacity infinite like nature.

If we are well informed, we understand that, as nature has graven her image and that of her Author on all things, they almost all partake of her double infinity. Thus we see that all the sciences are infinite in the extent of their researches. For who doubts that geometry, for instance, has an infinite infinity of problems to solve? They are also infinite in the multitude and fineness of their premises;

for it is clear that those which are put forward as ultimate are not self-supporting, but are based on others which, again having others for their support, do not permit of finality. But we represent some as ultimate for reason, in the same way as in regard to material objects we call that an indivisible point beyond which our senses can no longer perceive anything, although by its nature it is infinitely divisible.

Of these two Infinites of science, that of greatness is the most palpable, and hence a few persons have pretended to know all things. "I will speak of the whole," said Democritus.

But the infinitely little is the least obvious. Philosophers have much oftener claimed to have reached it, and it is here they have all stumbled. This has given rise to such common titles as First Principles, Principles of Philosophy, and the like, as ostentatious in fact, though not in appearance, as that one which blinds us, *De omni scibili*.[5]

We naturally believe ourselves far more capable of reaching the centre of things than of embracing their circumference. The visible extent of the world visibly exceeds us; but as we exceed little things, we think ourselves more capable of knowing them. And yet we need no less capacity for attaining the Nothing than the

All. Infinite capacity is required for both, and it seems to me that whoever shall have understood the ultimate principles of being might also attain to the knowledge of the Infinite. The one depends on the other, and one leads to the other. These extremes meet and reunite by force of distance and find each other in God, and in God alone.

Let us, then, take our compass; we are something, and we are not everything. The nature of our existence hides from us the knowledge of first beginnings which are born of the Nothing; and the littleness of our being conceals from us the sight of the Infinite.

Our intellect holds the same position in the world of thought as our body occupies in the expanse of nature.

Limited as we are in every way, this state which holds the mean between two extremes is present in all our impotence. Our senses perceive no extreme. Too much sound deafens us; too much light dazzles us; too great distance or proximity hinders our view. Too great length and too great brevity of discourse tend to obscurity; too much truth is paralysing (I know some who cannot understand that to take four from nothing leaves nothing). First principles are too self-evident for us; too much pleasure disagrees with us. Too many concords are annoying in music; too many benefits irritate us; we wish to have the wherewithal to overpay our debts. *Beneficia eo usque laeta sunt dum videntur exsolvi posse; ubi multum antevenere, pro gratia odium redditur.*[6] We feel neither extreme heat nor extreme cold. Excessive qualities are prejudicial to us and not perceptible by the senses; we do not feel but suffer them. Extreme youth and extreme age hinder the mind, as also too much and too little education. In short, extremes are for us as though they were not, and we are not within their notice. They escape us, or we them.

This is our true state; this is what makes us incapable of certain knowledge and of absolute ignorance. We sail within a vast sphere, ever drifting in uncertainty, driven from end to end. When we think to attach ourselves to any point and to fasten to it, it wavers and leaves us; and if we follow it, it eludes our grasp, slips past us, and vanishes for ever. Nothing stays for us. This is our natural condition and yet most contrary to our inclination; we burn with desire to find solid ground and an ultimate sure foundation whereon to build a tower reaching to the Infinite. But our whole groundwork cracks, and the earth opens to abysses.

Let us, therefore, not look for certainty and stability. Our reason is always deceived by fickle shadows; nothing can fix the finite between the two Infinites, which both enclose and fly from it.

If this be well understood, I think that we shall remain at rest, each in the state wherein nature has placed him. As this sphere which has fallen to us as our lot is always distant from either extreme, what matters it that man should have a little more knowledge of the universe? If he has it, he but gets a little higher. Is he not always infinitely removed from the end, and is not the duration of our life equally removed from eternity, even if it lasts ten years longer?

In comparison with these Infinites, all finites are equal, and I see no reason for fixing our imagination on one more than on another. The only comparison which we make of ourselves to the finite is painful to us.

If man made himself the first object of study, he would see how incapable he is of going further. How can a part know the whole? But he may perhaps aspire to know at least the parts to which he bears some proportion. But the parts of the world are all so related and linked to one another that I believe it impossible to know one without the other and without the whole.

Man, for instance, is related to all he knows. He needs a place wherein to abide, time through which to live, motion in order to live, elements to compose him, warmth and food to nourish him, air to breathe. He sees light; he feels bodies; in short, he is in a dependent alliance with everything. To know man, then, it is necessary to know how it happens that he needs air to live, and, to know the air, we must know how it is thus related to the life of man, etc. Flame cannot exist without air; therefore, to understand the one, we must understand the other.

Since everything, then, is cause and effect, dependent and supporting, mediate and immediate, and all is held together by a natural though imperceptible chain which binds together things most distant and most different, I hold it equally impossible to know the parts without knowing the whole and to know the whole without knowing the parts in detail.

The eternity of things in itself or in God must also astonish our brief duration. The fixed and constant immobility of nature, in comparison with the continual change which goes on within us, must have the same effect.

And what completes our incapability of knowing things is the fact that they are simple and that we are composed of two opposite natures, different in kind, soul and body. For it is impossible that our rational part should be other than spiritual; and if any one maintain that we are simply corporeal, this would far more exclude us from the knowledge of things, there being nothing so inconceivable as to say that matter knows itself. It is impossible to imagine how it should know itself.

So, if we are simply material, we can know nothing at all; and if we are composed of mind and matter, we cannot know perfectly things which are simple, whether spiritual or corporeal. Hence it comes that almost all philosophers have confused ideas of things, and speak of material things in spiritual terms, and of spiritual things in material terms. For they say boldly that bodies have a tendency to fall, that they seek after their centre, that they fly from destruction, that they fear the void, that they have inclinations, sympathies, antipathies, all of which attributes pertain only to mind. And in speaking of minds, they consider them as in a place, and attribute to them movement from one place to another; and these are qualities which belong only to bodies.

Instead of receiving the ideas of these things in their purity, we colour them with our own qualities, and stamp with our composite being all the simple things which we contemplate.

Who would not think, seeing us compose all things of mind and body, but that this mixture would be quite intelligible to us? Yet it is the very thing we least understand. Man is to himself the most wonderful object in nature; for he cannot conceive what the body is, still less what the mind is, and least of all how a body should be united to a mind. This is the consummation of his difficulties, and yet it is his very being. *Modus quo corporibus adhaerent spiritus comprehendi ab hominibus non potest, et hoc tamen homo est.*[7] Finally, to complete the proof of our weakness, I shall conclude with these two considerations...

73. But perhaps this subject goes beyond the capacity of reason. Let us therefore examine her solutions to problems within her powers. If there be anything to which her own interest must have made her apply herself most seriously, it is the inquiry into her own sovereign good. Let us see, then, wherein these strong and clear-sighted souls have placed it and whether they agree.

One says that the sovereign good consists in virtue, another in pleasure, another in the knowledge of nature, another in truth, *Felix qui potuit rerum cognoscere causas,*[8] another in total ignorance, another in indolence, others in disregarding appearances, another in wondering at nothing, *nihil admirari prope res una quae possit facere et servare beatum,*[9] and the true sceptics in their indifference, doubt, and perpetual suspense, and others, wiser, think to find a better definition. We are well satisfied.

We must see if this fine philosophy has gained nothing certain from so long and so intent study; perhaps at least the soul will know itself. Let us hear the rulers of the world on this subject. What have they thought of her substance? 394.[10] Have they been more fortunate in locating her? 395. What have they found out about her origin, duration, and departure? *Harum sententiarum*, 399.[11]

Is, then, the soul too noble a subject for their feeble lights? Let us, then, abase her to matter and see if she knows whereof is made the very body which she animates and those others which she contemplates and moves at her will. What have those great dogmatists, who are ignorant of nothing, known of this matter? 393.[12]

This would doubtless suffice, if Reason were reasonable. She is reasonable enough to admit that she has been unable to find anything durable, but she does not yet despair of reaching it; she is as ardent as ever in this search, and is confident she has within her the necessary powers for this conquest. We must therefore conclude, and, after having examined her powers in their effects, observe them in themselves, and see if she has a nature and a grasp capable of laying hold of the truth.

74. A letter On the Foolishness of Human Knowledge and Philosophy.
This letter before Diversion.
Felix qui potuit... Nihil admirari.

280 kinds of sovereign good in Montaigne.

75. Part I, 1, 2, c. 1, section 4.[13]

Probability.—It will not be difficult to put the case a stage lower, and make it appear ridiculous. To begin at the very beginning. What is more absurd than to say that lifeless bodies have passions, fears, hatreds—that insensible bodies, lifeless and incapable of life, have passions which presuppose at least a sensitive soul to feel them, nay more, that the object of their dread is the void? What is there in the void that could make them afraid? Nothing is more shallow and ridiculous. This is not all; it is said that they have in themselves a source of movement to shun the void. Have they arms, legs, muscles, nerves?

76. To write against those who made too profound a study of science: Descartes.

77. I cannot forgive Descartes. In all his philosophy he would have been quite willing to dispense with God. But he had to make Him give a fillip to set the world in motion; beyond this, he has no further need of God.

78. Descartes useless and uncertain.

79. Descartes.—We must say summarily: "This is made

by figure and motion," for it is true. But to say what these are, and to compose the machine, is ridiculous. For it is useless, uncertain, and painful. And were it true, we do not think all Philosophy is worth one hour of pain.

80. How comes it that a cripple does not offend us, but that a fool does? Because a cripple recognises that we walk straight, whereas a fool declares that it is we who are silly; if it were not so, we should feel pity and not anger.

Epictetus asks still more strongly: "Why are we not angry if we are told that we have a headache, and why are we angry if we are told that we reason badly, or choose wrongly"? The reason is that we are quite certain that we have not a headache, or are not lame, but we are not so sure that we make a true choice. So, having assurance only because we see with our whole sight, it puts us into suspense and surprise when another with his whole sight sees the opposite, and still more so when a thousand others deride our choice. For we must prefer our own lights to those of so many others, and that is bold and difficult. There is never this contradiction in the feelings towards a cripple.

81. It is natural for the mind to believe and for the will to love; so that, for want of true objects, they must attach themselves to false.

82. Imagination.—It is that deceitful part in man, that mistress of error and falsity, the more deceptive that she is not always so; for she would be an infallible rule of truth, if she were an infallible rule of falsehood. But being most generally false, she gives no sign of her nature, impressing the same character on the true and the false.

I do not speak of fools, I speak of the wisest men; and it is among them that the imagination has the great gift of persuasion. Reason protests in vain; it cannot set a true value on things.

This arrogant power, the enemy of reason, who likes to rule and dominate it, has established in man a second nature to show how all-powerful she is. She makes men happy and sad, healthy and sick, rich and poor; she compels reason to believe, doubt, and deny; she blunts the senses, or quickens them; she has her fools and sages; and nothing vexes us more than to see that she fills her devotees with a satisfaction far more full and entire than does reason. Those who have a lively imagination are a great deal more pleased with themselves than the wise can reasonably be. They look down upon men with haughtiness; they argue with boldness and confidence, others with fear and diffidence; and this gaiety of countenance often gives them the advantage in the opinion of the hearers, such favour have the imaginary wise in the eyes of judges of like nature. Imagination cannot make fools wise; but she can make them happy, to the envy of reason which can only make its friends miserable; the one covers them with glory, the other with shame.

What but this faculty of imagination dispenses reputation, awards respect and veneration to persons, works, laws, and the great? How insufficient are all the riches of the earth without her consent!

Would you not say that this magistrate, whose venerable age commands the respect of a whole people, is governed by pure and lofty reason, and that he judges causes according to their true nature without considering those mere trifles which only affect the imagination of the weak? See him go to sermon, full of devout zeal, strengthening his reason with the ardour of his love. He is ready to listen with exemplary respect. Let the preacher appear, and let nature have given him a hoarse voice or a comical cast of countenance, or let his barber have given him a bad shave, or let by chance his dress be more dirtied than usual, then, however great the truths he announces, I wager our senator loses his gravity.

If the greatest philosopher in the world find himself upon a plank wider than actually necessary, but hanging over a precipice, his imagination will prevail, though his reason convince him of his safety. Many cannot bear the thought without a cold sweat. I will not state all its effects.

Every one knows that the sight of cats or rats, the crushing of a coal, etc., may unhinge the reason. The tone of voice affects the wisest, and changes the force of a discourse or a poem.

Love or hate alters the aspect of justice. How much greater confidence has an advocate, retained with a large fee, in the justice of his cause! How much better does his bold manner make his case appear to the judges, deceived as they are by appearances! How ludicrous is reason, blown with a breath in every direction!

I should have to enumerate almost every action of men who scarce waver save under her assaults. For reason has been obliged to yield, and the wisest reason takes as her own principles those which the imagination of man has everywhere rashly introduced. He who would follow reason only would be deemed foolish by the generality of men. We must judge by the opinion of the majority of mankind. Because it has pleased them, we must work all day for pleasures seen to be imaginary; and, after sleep has refreshed our tired reason, we must forthwith start up and rush after phantoms, and suffer the impressions of this mistress of the world. This is one of the sources of error, but it is not the only one.

Our magistrates have known well this mystery. Their red robes, the ermine in which they wrap themselves like furry cats, the courts in which they administer justice, the fleurs-de-lis, and all such august apparel were necessary; if the physicians had not their cassocks and their mules, if the doctors had not their square caps and their robes four times too wide, they would never have duped the world, which cannot resist so original an appearance. If magistrates had true justice, and if physicians had the true art of healing, they would have no occasion for square caps; the majesty of these sciences would of itself be venerable enough. But having only imaginary knowledge, they must employ those silly tools that strike the imagination with which they have to deal; and thereby, in fact, they inspire respect. Soldiers alone are not disguised in this manner, because indeed their part is the most essential; they establish themselves by force, the others by show.

Therefore our kings seek out no disguises. They do not mask themselves in extraordinary costumes to appear such; but they are accompanied by guards and halberdiers. Those armed and red-faced puppets who have hands and power for them alone, those trumpets and drums which go before them, and those legions round about them, make the stoutest tremble. They have not dress only, they have might. A very refined reason is required to regard as an ordinary man the Grand Turk, in his superb seraglio, surrounded by forty thousand janissaries.

We cannot even see an advocate in his robe and with his cap on his head, without a favourable opinion of his ability. The imagination disposes of everything; it makes beauty, justice, and happiness, which is everything in the world. I should much like to see an Italian work, of which I only know the title, which alone is worth many books, *Della opinione regina del mondo*. I approve of the book without knowing it, save the evil in it, if any. These are pretty much the effects of that deceptive faculty, which seems to have been expressly given us to lead us into necessary error. We have, however, many other sources of error.

Not only are old impressions capable of misleading us; the charms of novelty have the same power. Hence arise all the disputes of men, who taunt each other either with following the false impressions of childhood or with running rashly after the new. Who keeps the due mean? Let him appear and prove it. There is no principle, however natural to us from infancy, which may not be made to pass for a false impression either of education or of sense.

"Because," say some, "you have believed from childhood that a box was empty when you saw nothing in it, you have believed in the possibility of a vacuum. This is an illusion of your senses, strengthened by custom, which science must correct." "Because," say others, "you have been taught at school that there is no vacuum, you have perverted your common sense which clearly comprehended it, and you must correct this by returning to your first state." Which has deceived you, your senses or your education?

We have another source of error in diseases. They spoil the judgement and the senses; and if the more serious produce a sensible change, I do not doubt that slighter ills produce a proportionate impression.

Our own interest is again a marvellous instrument for nicely putting out our eyes. The justest man in the world is not allowed to be judge in his own cause; I know some who, in order not to fall into this self-love, have been perfectly unjust out of opposition. The sure way of losing a just cause has been to get it recommended to these men by their near relatives.

Justice and truth are two such subtle points that our tools are too blunt to touch them accurately. If they reach the point, they either crush it, or lean all round, more on the false than on the true.

Man is so happily formed that he has no... good of the true, and several excellent of the false. Let us now see how much... But the most powerful cause of error is the war existing between the senses and reason.

83. We must thus begin the chapter on the deceptive powers. Man is only a subject full of error, natural and ineffaceable, without grace. Nothing shows him the truth. Everything deceives him. These two sources of truth, reason and the senses, besides being both wanting in sincerity, deceive each other in turn. The senses mislead the Reason with false appearances, and receive from Reason in their turn the same trickery which they apply to her; Reason has her revenge. The passions of the soul trouble the senses, and make false impressions upon them. They rival each other in falsehood and deception.

But besides those errors which arise accidentally and through lack of intelligence, with these heterogeneous faculties...

84. The imagination enlarges little objects so as to fill our souls with a fantastic estimate; and, with rash insolence, it belittles the great to its own measure, as when talking of God.

85. Things which have most hold on us, as the

concealment of our few possessions, are often a mere nothing. It is a nothing which our imagination magnifies into a mountain. Another turn of the imagination would make us discover this without difficulty.

86. My fancy makes me hate a croaker, and one who pants when eating. Fancy has great weight. Shall we profit by it? Shall we yield to this weight because it is natural? No, but by resisting it...

87. *Nae iste magno conatu magnas nugas dixerit.*[14] 583.[15] *Quasi quidquam infelicius sit homini cui sua figmenta dominantur.*[16]

88. Children who are frightened at the face they have blackened are but children. But how shall one who is so weak in his childhood become really strong when he grows older? We only change our fancies. All that is made perfect by progress perishes also by progress. All that has been weak can never become absolutely strong. We say in vain, "He has grown, he has changed"; he is also the same.

89. Custom is our nature. He who is accustomed to the faith believes in it, can no longer fear hell, and believes in nothing else. He who is accustomed to believe that the king is terrible... etc. Who doubts, then, that our soul, being accustomed to see number, space, motion,

believes that and nothing else?

90. *Quod crebro videt non miratur, etiamsi cur fiat nescit; quod ante non viderit, id si evenerit, ostentum esse censet.*[17]

91. *Spongia solis.*—When we see the same effect always recur, we infer a natural necessity in it, as that there will be a tomorrow, etc. But Nature often deceives us, and does not subject herself to her own rules.

92. What are our natural principles but principles of custom? In children they are those which they have received from the habits of their fathers, as hunting in animals. A different custom will cause different natural principles. This is seen in experience; and if there are some natural principles ineradicable by custom, there are also some customs opposed to nature, ineradicable by nature or by a second custom. This depends on disposition.

93. Parents fear lest the natural love of their children may fade away. What kind of nature is that which is subject to decay? Custom is a second nature which destroys the former. But what is nature? For is custom not natural? I am much afraid that nature is itself only a first custom, as custom is a second nature.

94. The nature of man is wholly natural, *omne animal.*[18]

There is nothing he may not make natural; there is nothing natural he may not lose.

95. Memory, joy, are intuitions; and even mathematical propositions become intuitions, for education produces natural intuitions, and natural intuitions are erased by education.

96. When we are accustomed to use bad reasons for proving natural effects, we are not willing to receive good reasons when they are discovered. An example may be given from the circulation of the blood as a reason why the vein swells below the ligature.

97. The most important affair in life is the choice of a calling; chance decides it. Custom makes men masons, soldiers, slaters. "He is a good slater," says one, and, speaking of soldiers, remarks, "They are perfect fools." But others affirm, "There is nothing great but war; the rest of men are good for nothing." We choose our callings according as we hear this or that praised or despised in our childhood, for we naturally love truth and hate folly. These words move us; the only error is in their application. So great is the force of custom that, out of those whom nature has only made men, are created all conditions of men. For some districts are full of masons, others of soldiers, etc. Certainly nature is not so uniform. It is custom then which does this,

for it constrains nature. But sometimes nature gains the ascendancy and preserves man's instinct, in spite of all custom, good or bad.

98. Bias leading to error.—It is a deplorable thing to see all men deliberating on means alone, and not on the end. Each thinks how he will acquit himself in his condition; but as for the choice of condition, or of country, chance gives them to us.

It is a pitiable thing to see so many Turks, heretics, and infidels follow the way of their fathers for the sole reason that each has been imbued with the prejudice that it is the best. And that fixes for each man his condition of locksmith, soldier, etc.

Hence savages care nothing for Providence.

99. There is an universal and essential difference between the actions of the will and all other actions.

The will is one of the chief factors in belief, not that it creates belief, but because things are true or false according to the aspect in which we look at them. The will, which prefers one aspect to another, turns away the mind from considering the qualities of all that it does not like to see; and thus the mind, moving in accord with the will, stops to consider the aspect which it likes and so judges by what it sees.

100. Self-love. The nature of self-love and of this human Ego is to love self only and consider self only. But what will man do? He cannot prevent this object that he loves from being full of faults and wants. He wants to be great, and he sees himself small. He wants to be happy, and he sees himself miserable. He wants to be perfect, and he sees himself full of imperfections. He wants to be the object of love and esteem among men, and he sees that his faults merit only their hatred and contempt. This embarrassment in which he finds himself produces in him the most unrighteous and criminal passion that can be imagined; for he conceives a mortal enmity against that truth which reproves him and which convinces him of his faults. He would annihilate it, but, unable to destroy it in its essence, he destroys it as far as possible in his own knowledge and in that of others; that is to say, he devotes all his attention to hiding his faults both from others and from himself, and he cannot endure either that others should point them out to him, or that they should see them.

Truly it is an evil to be full of faults; but it is a still greater evil to be full of them and to be unwilling to recognise them, since that is to add the further fault of a voluntary illusion. We do not like others to deceive us; we do not think it fair that they should be held in higher esteem by us than they deserve; it is not, then, fair that we should deceive them and should wish them to esteem us more highly than we deserve.

Thus, when they discover only the imperfections and vices which we really have, it is plain they do us no wrong, since it is not they who cause them; they rather do us good, since they help us to free ourselves from an evil, namely, the ignorance of these imperfections. We ought not to be angry at their knowing our faults and despising us; it is but right that they should know us for what we are and should despise us, if we are contemptible.

Such are the feelings that would arise in a heart full of equity and justice. What must we say then of our own heart, when we see it in a wholly different disposition? For is it not true that we hate truth and those who tell it us, and that we like them to be deceived in our favour, and prefer to be esteemed by them as being other than what we are in fact? One proof of this makes me shudder. The Catholic religion does not bind us to confess our sins indiscriminately to everybody; it allows them to remain hidden from all other men save one, to whom she bids us reveal the innermost recesses of our heart and show ourselves as we are. There is only this one man in the world whom she orders us to undeceive, and she binds him to an inviolable secrecy, which makes this knowledge to him as if it were not. Can we imagine anything more charitable and pleasant? And yet the corruption of man is such that he finds even this law harsh; and it is one of the main reasons which has caused a great part of Europe to rebel against the Church.

How unjust and unreasonable is the heart of man, which feels it disagreeable to be obliged to do in regard to one man what in some measure it were right to do to all men! For is it right that we should deceive men?

There are different degrees in this aversion to truth; but all may perhaps be said to have it in some degree, because it is inseparable from self-love. It is this false delicacy which makes those who are under the necessity of reproving others choose so many windings and middle courses to avoid offence. They must lessen our faults, appear to excuse them, intersperse praises and evidence of love and esteem. Despite all this, the medicine does not cease to be bitter to self-love. It takes as little as it can, always with disgust, and often with a secret spite against those who administer it.

Hence it happens that, if any have some interest in being loved by us, they are averse to render us a service which they know to be disagreeable. They treat us as we wish to be treated. We hate the truth, and they hide it from us. We desire flattery, and they flatter us. We like to be deceived, and they deceive us.

So each degree of good fortune which raises us in the world removes us farther from truth, because we are most afraid of wounding those whose affection is most useful and whose dislike is most dangerous. A prince may be the byword of all Europe, and he alone will know nothing of it. I am not astonished. To tell the truth is useful to those to whom it is spoken, but disadvantageous to those who tell it, because it makes them disliked. Now those who live with princes love their own interests more than that of the prince whom they serve; and so they take care not to confer on him a benefit so as to injure themselves.

This evil is no doubt greater and more common among the higher classes; but the lower are not exempt from it, since there is always some advantage in making men love us. Human life is thus only a perpetual illusion; men deceive and flatter each other. No one speaks of us in our presence as he does of us in our absence. Human society is founded on mutual deceit; few friendships would endure if each knew what his friend said of him in his absence, although he then spoke in sincerity and without passion.

Man is, then, only disguise, falsehood, and hypocrisy, both in himself and in regard to others. He does not wish any one to tell him the truth; he avoids telling it to others, and all these dispositions, so removed from justice and reason, have a natural root in his heart.

101. I set it down as a fact that if all men knew what each said of the other, there would not be four friends in the world. This is apparent from the quarrels which arise from the indiscreet tales told from time to time. I say, further, all men would be...

102. Some vices only lay hold of us by means of others, and these, like branches, fall on removal of the trunk.

103. The example of Alexander's chastity has not made so many continent as that of his drunkenness has made intemperate. It is not shameful not to be as virtuous as he, and it seems excusable to be no more vicious. We do not believe ourselves to be exactly sharing in the vices of the vulgar when we see that we are sharing in those of great men; and yet we do not observe that in these matters they are ordinary men. We hold on to them by the same end by which they hold on to the rabble; for, however exalted they are, they are still united at some point to the lowest of men. They are not suspended in the air, quite removed from our society. No, no; if they are greater than we, it is because their heads are higher; but their feet are as low as ours. They are all on the same level, and rest on the same earth; and by that extremity they are as low as we are, as the meanest folk, as infants, and as the beasts.

104. When our passion leads us to do something, we

forget our duty; for example, we like a book and read it, when we ought to be doing something else. Now, to remind ourselves of our duty, we must set ourselves a task we dislike; we then plead that we have something else to do and by this means remember our duty.

105. How difficult it is to submit anything to the judgement of another, without prejudicing his judgement by the manner in which we submit it! If we say, "I think it beautiful," "I think it obscure," or the like, we either entice the imagination into that view, or irritate it to the contrary. It is better to say nothing; and then the other judges according to what really is, that is to say, according as it then is and according as the other circumstances, not of our making, have placed it. But we at least shall have added nothing, unless it be that silence also produces an effect, according to the turn and the interpretation which the other will be disposed to give it, or as he will guess it from gestures or countenance, or from the tone of the voice, if he is a physiognomist. So difficult is it not to upset a judgement from its natural place, or, rather, so rarely is it firm and stable!

106. By knowing each man's ruling passion, we are sure of pleasing him; and yet each has his fancies, opposed to his true good, in the very idea which he has of the good. It is a singularly puzzling fact.

107. *Lustravit lampade terras.*[19]—The weather and my mood have little connection. I have my foggy and my fine days within me; my prosperity or misfortune has little to do with the matter. I sometimes struggle against luck, the glory of mastering it makes me master it gaily; whereas I am sometimes surfeited in the midst of good fortune.

108. Although people may have no interest in what they are saying, we must not absolutely conclude from this that they are not lying; for there are some people who lie for the mere sake of lying.

109. When we are well we wonder what we would do if we were ill, but when we are ill we take medicine cheerfully; the illness persuades us to do so. We have no longer the passions and desires for amusements and promenades which health gave to us, but which are incompatible with the necessities of illness. Nature gives us, then, passions and desires suitable to our present state. We are only troubled by the fears which we, and not nature, give ourselves, for they add to the state in which we are the passions of the state in which we are not.

As nature makes us always unhappy in every state, our desires picture to us a happy state; because they add to the state in which we are the pleasures of the state in which we are not. And if we attained to these pleasures, we should not be happy after all; because we should have other desires natural to this new state.

We must particularise this general proposition....

110. The consciousness of the falsity of present pleasures, and the ignorance of the vanity of absent pleasures, cause inconstancy.

111. Inconstancy.—We think we are playing on ordinary organs when playing upon man. Men are organs, it is true, but, odd, changeable, variable with pipes not arranged in proper order. Those who only know how to play on ordinary organs will not produce barmonies on these. We must know where are.

112. Inconstancy.—Things have different qualities, and the soul different inclinations; for nothing is simple which is presented to the soul, and the soul never presents itself simply to any object. Hence it comes that we weep and laugh at the same thing.

113. Inconstancy and oddity.—To live only by work, and to rule over the most powerful State in the world, are very opposite things. They are united in the person of the great Sultan of the Turks.

114. Variety is as abundant as all tones of the voice, all

ways of walking, coughing, blowing the nose, sneezing. We distinguish vines by their fruit, and call them the Condrien, the Desargues, and such and such a stock. Is this all? Has a vine ever produced two bunches exactly the same, and has a bunch two grapes alike, etc.?

I can never judge of the same thing exactly in the same way. I cannot judge of my work, while doing it. I must do as the artists, stand at a distance, but not too far. How far, then? Guess.

115. Variety.—Theology is a science, but at the same time how many sciences? A man is a whole; but if we dissect him, will he be the head, the heart, the stomach, the veins, each vein, each portion of a vein, the blood, each humour in the blood?

A town, a country-place, is from afar a town and a country-place. But, as we draw near, there are houses, trees, tiles, leaves, grass, ants, limbs of ants, in infinity. All this is contained under the name of country-place.

116. Thoughts.—All is one, all is different. How many natures exist in man? How many vocations? And by what chance does each man ordinarily choose what he has heard praised? A well-turned heel.

117. The heel of a slipper.—"Ah! How well this is

turned! Here is a clever workman! How brave is this soldier!" This is the source of our inclinations and of the choice of conditions. "How much this man drinks! How little that one"! This makes people sober or drunk, soldiers, cowards, etc.

118. Chief talent, that which rules the rest.

119. Nature imitates herself A seed grown in good ground brings forth fruit. A principle instilled into a good mind brings forth fruit. Numbers imitate space, which is of a different nature.

All is made and led by the same master, root, branches, and fruits; principles and consequences.

120. Nature diversifies and imitates; art imitates and diversifies.

121. Nature always begins the same things again, the years, the days, the hours; in like manner spaces and numbers follow each other from beginning to end. Thus is made a kind of infinity and eternity. Not that anything in all this is infinite and eternal, but these finite realities are infinitely multiplied. Thus it seems to me to be only the number which multiplies them that is infinite.

122. Time heals griefs and quarrels, for we change and are no longer the same persons. Neither the offender nor the offended are any more themselves. It is like a nation which we have provoked, but meet again after two generations. They are still Frenchmen, but not the same.

123. He no longer loves the person whom he loved ten years ago. I quite believe it. She is no longer the same, nor is he. He was young, and she also; she is quite different. He would perhaps love her yet, if she were what she was then.

124. We view things not only from different sides, but with different eyes; we have no wish to find them alike.

125. Contraries.—Man is naturally credulous and incredulous, timid and rash.

126. Description of man: dependency, desire of independence, need.

127. Condition of man: inconstancy, weariness, unrest.

128. The weariness which is felt by us in leaving pursuits to which we are attached. A man dwells at home with pleasure; but if he sees a woman who charms him,

or if he enjoys himself in play for five or six days, he is miserable if he returns to his former way of living. Nothing is more common than that.

129. Our nature consists in motion; complete rest is death.

130. Restlessness.—If a soldier, or labourer, complain of the hardship of his lot, set him to do nothing.

131. Weariness.—Nothing is so insufferable to man as to be completely at rest, without passions, without business, without diversion, without study. He then feels his nothingness, his forlornness, his insufficiency, his dependence, his weakness, his emptiness. There will immediately arise from the depth of his heart weariness, gloom, sadness, fretfulness, vexation, despair.

132. Methinks Caesar was too old to set about amusing himself with conquering the world. Such sport was good for Augustus or Alexander. They were still young men and thus difficult to restrain. But Caesar should have been more mature.

133. Two faces which resemble each other make us laugh, when together, by their resemblance, though neither of them by itself makes us laugh.

134. How useless is painting, which attracts admiration by the resemblance of things, the originals of which we do not admire!

135. The struggle alone pleases us, not the victory. We love to see animals fighting, not the victor infuriated over the vanquished. We would only see the victorious end; and, as soon as it comes, we are satiated. It is the same in play, and the same in the search for truth. In disputes we like to see the clash of opinions, but not at all to contemplate truth when found. To observe it with pleasure, we have to see it emerge out of strife. So in the passions, there is pleasure in seeing the collision of two contraries; but when one acquires the mastery, it becomes only brutality. We never seek things for themselves, but for the search. Likewise in plays, scenes which do not rouse the emotion of fear are worthless, so are extreme and hopeless misery, brutal lust, and extreme cruelty.

136. A mere trifle consoles us, for a mere trifle distresses us.

137. Without examining every particular pursuit, it is enough to comprehend them under diversion.

138. Men naturally slaters and of all callings, save in their own rooms.

139. Diversion.—When I have occasionally set myself to consider the different distractions of men, the pains and perils to which they expose themselves at court or in war, whence arise so many quarrels, passions, bold and often bad ventures, etc., I have discovered that all the unhappiness of men arises from one single fact, that they cannot stay quietly in their own chamber. A man who has enough to live on, if he knew how to stay with pleasure at home, would not leave it to go to sea or to besiege a town. A commission in the army would not be bought so dearly, but that it is found insufferable not to budge from the town; and men only seek conversation and entering games, because they cannot remain with pleasure at home.

But, on further consideration, when, after finding the cause of all our ills, I have sought to discover the reason of it, I have found that there is one very real reason, namely, the natural poverty of our feeble and mortal condition, so miserable that nothing can comfort us when we think of it closely.

Whatever condition we picture to ourselves, if we muster all the good things which it is possible to possess, royalty is the finest position in the world. Yet, when we imagine a king attended with every pleasure he can feel, if he be without diversion and be left to consider and reflect on what he is, this feeble happiness will not sustain him; he will necessarily fall into forebodings of dangers, of revolutions which may happen, and, finally, of death and inevitable disease; so that, if he be without what is called diversion, he is unhappy and more unhappy than the least of his subjects who plays and diverts himself.

Hence it comes that play and the society of women, war and high posts, are so sought after. Not that there is in fact any happiness in them, or that men imagine true bliss to consist in money won at play, or in the hare which they hunt; we would not take these as a gift. We do not seek that easy and peaceful lot which permits us to think of our unhappy condition, nor the dangers of war, nor the labour of office, but the bustle which averts these thoughts of ours and amuses us.

Reasons why we like the chase better than the quarry.

Hence it comes that men so much love noise and stir; hence it comes that the prison is so horrible a punishment; hence it comes that the pleasure of solitude is a thing incomprehensible. And it is, in fact, the greatest source of happiness in the condition of kings that men try incessantly to divert them and to procure for them all kinds of pleasures.

The king is surrounded by persons whose only thought is to divert the king and to prevent his thinking of self.

For he is unhappy, king though he be, if he think of himself.

This is all that men have been able to discover to make themselves happy. And those who philosophise on the matter, and who think men unreasonable for spending a whole day in chasing a hare which they would not have bought, scarce know our nature. The hare in itself would not screen us from the sight of death and calamities; but the chase, which turns away our attention from these, does screen us.

The advice given to Pyrrhus, to take the rest which he was about to seek with so much labour, was full of difficulties.

To bid a man live quietly is to bid him live happily. It is to advise him to be in a state perfectly happy, in which he can think at leisure without finding therein a cause of distress. This is to misunderstand nature.

As men who naturally understand their own condition avoid nothing so much as rest, so there is nothing they leave undone in seeking turmoil. Not that they have an instinctive knowledge of true happiness...

So we are wrong in blaming them. Their error does not lie in seeking excitement, if they seek it only as a diversion; the evil is that they seek it as if the possession of the objects of their quest would make them really happy. In this respect it is right to call their quest a vain one. Hence in all this both the censurers and the censured do not understand man's true nature.

And thus, when we take the exception against them, that what they seek with such fervour cannot satisfy them, if they replied—as they should do if they considered the matter thoroughly—that they sought in it only a violent and impetuous occupation which turned their thoughts from self, and that they therefore chose an attractive object to charm and ardently attract them, they would leave their opponents without a reply. But they do not make this reply, because they do not know themselves. They do not know that it is the chase, and not the quarry, which they seek.

Dancing: We must consider rightly where to place our feet.—A gentleman sincerely believes that hunting is great and royal sport; but a beater is not of this opinion.

They imagine that, if they obtained such a post, they would then rest with pleasure and are insensible of the insatiable nature of the if desire. They think they are truly seeking quiet, and they are only seeking excitement.

They have a secret instinct which impels them to seek amusement and occupation abroad, and which arises from the sense of their constant unhappiness. They have another secret instinct, a remnant of the greatness of our original nature, which teaches them that happiness in reality consists only in rest and not in stir. And of these two contrary instincts they form within themselves a confused idea, which hides itself from their view in the depths of their soul, inciting them to aim at rest through excitement, and always to fancy that the satisfaction which they have not will come to them, if, by surmounting whatever difficulties confront them, they can thereby open the door to rest.

Thus passes away all man's life. Men seek rest in a struggle against difficulties; and when they have conquered these, rest becomes insufferable. For we think either of the misfortunes we have or of those which threaten us. And even if we should see ourselves sufficiently sheltered on all sides, weariness of its own accord would not fail to arise from the depths of the heart wherein it has its natural roots and to fill the mind with its poison.

Thus so wretched is man that he would weary even without any cause for weariness from the peculiar state of his disposition; and so frivolous is he that, though full of a thousand reasons for weariness, the least thing, such as playing billiards or hitting a ball, is sufficient to amuse him.

But will you say what object has he in all this? The pleasure of bragging tomorrow among his friends that he has played better than another. So others sweat in their own rooms to show to the learned that they have solved a problem in algebra, which no one had hitherto been able to solve. Many more expose themselves to extreme perils, in my opinion as foolishly, in order to boast afterwards that they have captured a town. Lastly, others wear themselves out in studying all these things, not in order to become wiser, but only in order to prove that they know them; and these are the most senseless of the band, since they are so knowingly, whereas one may suppose of the others that, if they knew it, they would no longer be foolish.

This man spends his life without weariness in playing every day for a small stake. Give him each morning the money he can win each day, on condition he does not play; you make him miserable. It will perhaps be said that he seeks the amusement of play and not the winnings. Make him, then, play for nothing; he will not become excited over it and will feel bored. It is, then, not the amusement alone that he seeks; a languid and passionless amusement will weary him. He must get excited over it and deceive himself by the fancy that he will be happy to win what he would not have as a gift on condition of not playing; and he must make for himself an object of passion, and excite over it his desire, his anger, his fear, to obtain his imagined end, as children are frightened at the face they have blackened.

Whence comes it that this man, who lost his only son a few months ago, or who this morning was in such trouble through being distressed by lawsuits and quarrels, now no longer thinks of them? Do not wonder; he is quite taken up in looking out for the boar which his dogs have been hunting so hotly for the last six hours. He requires nothing more. However full of sadness a man may be, he is happy for the time, if you can prevail upon him to enter into some amusement; and however happy a man may be, he will soon be discontented and wretched, if he be not diverted and occupied by some passion or pursuit which prevents weariness from overcoming him. Without amusement there is no joy; with amusement there is no sadness. And this also constitutes the happiness of persons in high position, that they have a number of people to amuse them and have the power to keep themselves in this state.

Consider this. What is it to be superintendent, chancellor, first president, but to be in a condition wherein from early morning a large number of people come from all quarters to see them, so as not to leave them an hour in the day in which they can think of themselves? And when they are in disgrace and sent back to their country houses, where they lack neither wealth nor servants to help them on occasion, they do not fail to be wretched and desolate, because no one prevents them from thinking of themselves.

140. How does it happen that this man, so distressed at the death of his wife and his only son, or who has some great lawsuit which annoys him, is not at this moment sad, and that he seems so free from all painful and disquieting thoughts? We need not wonder; for a ball has been served him, and he must return it to his companion. He is occupied in catching it in its fall from the roof, to win a game. How can he think of his own affairs, pray, when he has this other matter in hand? Here is a care worthy of occupying this great soul and taking away from him every other thought of the mind. This man, born to know the universe, to judge all causes, to govern a whole state, is altogether occupied and taken up with the business of catching a hare. And if he does not lower himself to this and wants always to be on the strain, he will be more foolish still, because he would raise himself above humanity; and after all, he is only a man, that is to say capable of little and of much, of all and of nothing; he is neither angel nor brute, but man.

141. Men spend their time in following a ball or a hare; it is the pleasure even of kings.

142. Diversion—Is not the royal dignity sufficiently

great in itself to make its possessor happy by the mere contemplation of what he is? Must he be diverted from this thought like ordinary folk? I see well that a man is made happy by diverting him from the view of his domestic sorrows so as to occupy all his thoughts with the care of dancing well. But will it be the same with a king, and will he be happier in the pursuit of these idle amusements than in the contemplation of his greatness? And what more satisfactory object could be presented to his mind? Would it not be a deprivation of his delight for him to occupy his soul with the thought of how to adjust his steps to the cadence of an air, or of how to throw a ball skilfully, instead of leaving it to enjoy quietly the contemplation of the majestic glory which encompasses him? Let us make the trial; let us leave a king all alone to reflect on himself quite at leisure, without any gratification of the senses, without any care in his mind, without society; and we will see that a king without diversion is a man full of wretchedness. So this is carefully avoided, and near the persons of kings there never fail to be a great number of people who see to it that amusement follows business, and who watch all the time of their leisure to supply them with delights and games, so that there is no blank in it. In fact, kings are surrounded with persons who are wonderfully attentive in taking care that the king be not alone and in a state to think of himself, knowing well that he will be miserable, king though he be, if he meditate on self.

In all this I am not talking of Christian kings as Christians, but only as kings.

143. Diversion.—Men are entrusted from infancy with the care of their honour, their property, their friends, and even with the property and the honour of their friends. They are overwhelmed with business, with the study of languages, and with physical exercise; and they are made to understand that they cannot be happy unless their health, their honour, their fortune and that of their friends be in good condition, and that a single thing wanting will make them unhappy. Thus they are given cares and business which make them bustle about from break of day. It is, you will exclaim, a strange way to make them happy! What more could be done to make them miserable?—Indeed! what could be done? We should only have to relieve them from all these cares; for then they would see themselves: they would reflect on what they are, whence they came, whither they go, and thus we cannot employ and divert them too much. And this is why, after having given them so much business, we advise them, if they have some time for relaxation, to employ it in amusement, in play, and to be always fully occupied.

How hollow and full of ribaldry is the heart of man!

144. I spent a long time in the study of the abstract

sciences, and was disheartened by the small number of fellow-students in them. When I commenced the study of man, I saw that these abstract sciences are not suited to man and that I was wandering farther from my own state in examining them than others in not knowing them. I pardoned their little knowledge; but I thought at least to find many companions in the study of man and that it was the true study which is suited to him. I have been deceived; still fewer study it than geometry. It is only from the want of knowing how to study this that we seek the other studies. But is it not that even here is not the knowledge which man should have and that for the purpose of happiness it is better for him not to know himself?

145. One thought alone occupies us; we cannot think of two things at the same time. This is lucky for us according to the world, not according to God.

146. Man is obviously made to think. It is his whole dignity and his whole merit; and his whole duty is to think as he ought. Now, the order of thought is to begin with self, and with its Author and its end.

Now, of what does the world think? Never of this, but of dancing, playing the lute, singing, making verses, running at the ring, etc., fighting, making oneself king, without thinking what it is to be a king and what to be a man.

147. We do not content ourselves with the life we have in ourselves and in our own being; we desire to live an imaginary life in the mind of others, and for this purpose we endeavour to shine. We labour unceasingly to adorn and preserve this imaginary existence and neglect the real. And if we possess calmness, or generosity, or truthfulness, we are eager to make it known, so as to attach these virtues to that imaginary existence. We would rather separate them from ourselves to join them to it; and we would willingly be cowards in order to acquire the reputation of being brave. A great proof of the nothingness of our being, not to be satisfied with the one without the other, and to renounce the one for the other! For he would be infamous who would not die to preserve his honour.

148. We are so presumptuous that we would wish to be known by all the world, even by people who shall come after, when we shall be no more; and we are so vain that the esteem of five or six neighbours delights and contents us.

149. We do not trouble ourselves about being esteemed in the towns through which we pass. But if we are to remain a little while there, we are so concerned. How long is necessary? A time commensurate with our vain and paltry life.

150. Vanity is so anchored in the heart of man that a soldier, a soldier's servant, a cook, a porter brags and wishes to have his admirers. Even philosophers wish for them. Those who write against it want to have the glory of having written well; and those who read it desire the glory of having read it. I who write this have perhaps this desire, and perhaps those who will read it...

151. Glory.—Admiration spoils all from infancy. Ah! How well said! Ah! How well done! How well-behaved he is! etc.

The children of Port-Royal, who do not receive this stimulus of envy and glory, fall into carelessness.

152. Pride.—Curiosity is only vanity. Most frequently we wish to know but to talk. Otherwise we would not take a sea voyage in order never to talk of it, and for the sole pleasure of seeing without hope of ever communicating it.

153. Of the desire of being esteemed by those with whom we are.—Pride takes such natural possession of us in the midst of our woes, errors, etc. We even lose our life with joy, provided people talk of it.

Vanity: play, hunting, visiting, false shame, a lasting name.

154. I have no friends to your advantage.

155. A true friend is so great an advantage, even for the greatest lords, in order that he may speak well of them and back them in their absence, that they should do all to have one. But they should choose well; for, if they spend all their efforts in the interests of fools, it will be of no use, however well these may speak of them; and these will not even speak well of them if they find themselves on the weakest side, for they have no influence; and thus they will speak ill of them in company.

156. *Ferox gens, nullam esse vitam sine armis rati.*[20]—They prefer death to peace; others prefer death to war.

Every opinion may be held preferable to life, the love of which is so strong and so natural.

157. Contradiction: contempt for our existence, to die for nothing, hatred of our existence.

158. Pursuits.—The charm of fame is so great that we like every object to which it is attached, even death.

159. Noble deeds are most estimable when hidden. When I see some of these in history, they please me greatly. But after all they have not been quite hidden, since they have been known; and though people have

done what they could to hide them, the little publication of them spoils all, for what was best in them was the wish to hide them.

160. Sneezing absorbs all the functions of the soul, as well as work does; but we do not draw therefrom the same conclusions against the greatness of man, because it is against his will. And although we bring it on ourselves, it is nevertheless against our will that we sneeze. It is not in view of the act itself; it is for another end. And thus it is not a proof of the weakness of man and of his slavery under that action.

It is not disgraceful for man to yield to pain, and it is disgraceful to yield to pleasure. This is not because pain comes to us from without, and we ourselves seek pleasure; for it is possible to seek pain, and yield to it purposely, without this kind of baseness. Whence comes it, then, that reason thinks it honourable to succumb under stress of pain, and disgraceful to yield to the attack of pleasure? It is because pain does not tempt and attract us. It is we ourselves who choose it voluntarily, and will it to prevail over us. So that we are masters of the situation; and in this man yields to himself. But in pleasure it is man who yields to pleasure. Now only mastery and sovereignty bring glory, and only slavery brings shame.

161. Vanity.—How wonderful it is that a thing so evident as the vanity of the world is so little known, that it is a strange and surprising thing to say that it is foolish to seek greatness?

162. He who will know fully the vanity of man has only to consider the causes and effects of love. The cause is a *je ne sais quoi* (Corneille), and the effects are dreadful. This *je ne sais quoi*, so small an object that we cannot recognise it, agitates a whole country, princes, armies, the entire world.

Cleopatra's nose: had it been shorter, the whole aspect of the world would have been altered.

163. Vanity.—The cause and the effects of love: Cleopatra.

164. He who does not see the vanity of the world is himself very vain. Indeed who do not see it but youths who are absorbed in fame, diversion, and the thought of the future? But take away diversion, and you will see them dried up with weariness. They feel then their nothingness without knowing it; for it is indeed to be unhappy to be in insufferable sadness as soon as we are reduced to thinking of self and have no diversion.

165. Thoughts.—*In omnibus requiem quaesivi.*[21] If our

condition were truly happy, we not need diversion from thinking of it in order to make ourselves happy.

166. Diversion.—Death is easier to bear without thinking of it than is the thought of death without peril.

167. The miseries of human life has established all this: as men have seen this, they have taken up diversion.

168. Diversion.—As men are not able to fight against death, misery, ignorance, they have taken it into their heads, in order to be happy, not to think of them at all.

169. Despite these miseries, man wishes to be happy, and only wishes to be happy, and cannot wish not to be so. But how will he set about it? To be happy he would have to make himself immortal; but, not being able to do so, it has occurred to him to prevent himself from thinking of death.

170. Diversion.—If man were happy, he would be the more so, the less he was diverted, like the Saints and God. Yes; but is it not to be happy to have a faculty of being amused by diversion? No; for that comes from elsewhere and from without, and thus is dependent, and therefore subject to be disturbed by a thousand accidents, which bring inevitable griefs.

171. Misery.—The only thing which consoles us for our miseries is diversion, and yet this is the greatest of our miseries. For it is this which principally hinders us from reflecting upon ourselves and which makes us insensibly ruin ourselves. Without this we should be in a state of weariness, and this weariness would spur us to seek a more solid means of escaping from it. But diversion amuses us, and leads us unconsciously to death.

172. We do not rest satisfied with the present. We anticipate the future as too slow in coming, as if in order to hasten its course; or we recall the past, to stop its too rapid flight. So imprudent are we that we wander in the times which are not ours and do not think of the only one which belongs to us; and so idle are we that we dream of those times which are no more and thoughtlessly overlook that which alone exists. For the present is generally painful to us. We conceal it from our sight, because it troubles us; and, if it be delightful to us, we regret to see it pass away. We try to sustain it by the future and think of arranging matters which are not in our power, for a time which we have no certainty of reaching.

Let each one examine his thoughts, and he will find them all occupied with the past and the future. We scarcely ever think of the present; and if we think of it, it is only to take light from it to arrange the future. The present is never our end. The past and the present are our means; the future alone is our end. So we never live, but we hope to live; and, as we are always preparing to be happy, it is inevitable we should never be so.

173. They say that eclipses foretoken misfortune, because misfortunes are common, so that, as evil happens so often, they often foretell it; whereas if they said that they predict good fortune, they would often be wrong. They attribute good fortune only to rare conjunctions of the heavens; so they seldom fail in prediction.

174. Misery.—Solomon and Job have best known and best spoken of the misery of man; the former the most fortunate, and the latter the most unfortunate of men; the former knowing the vanity of pleasures from experience, the latter the reality of evils.

175. We know ourselves so little that many think they are about to die when they are well, and many think they are well when they are near death, unconscious of approaching fever, or of the abscess ready to form itself.

176. Cromwell was about to ravage all Christendom; the royal family was undone, and his own for ever established, save for a little grain of sand which formed in his ureter. Rome herself was trembling under him; but this small piece of gravel having formed there, he is

dead, his family cast down, all is peaceful, and the king is restored.

177. Three hosts. Would he who had possessed the friendship of the King of England, the King of Poland, and the Queen of Sweden, have believed he would lack a refuge and shelter in the world?

178. Macrobius: on the innocents slain by Herod.

179. When Augustus learnt that Herod's own son was amongst the infants under two years of age, whom he had caused to be slain, he said that it was better to be Herod's pig than his son. Macrobius, Saturnalia, ii. 4.

180. The great and the humble have the same misfortunes, the same griefs, the same passions; but the one is at the top of the wheel, and the other near the centre, and so less disturbed by the same revolutions.

181. We are so unfortunate that we can only take pleasure in a thing on condition of being annoyed if it turn out ill, as a thousand things can do, and do every hour. He who should find the secret of rejoicing in the good, without troubling himself with its contrary evil, would have hit the mark. It is perpetual motion.

182. Those who have always good hope in the midst of

misfortunes, and who are delighted with good luck, are suspected of being very pleased with the ill success of the affair, if they are not equally distressed by bad luck; and they are overjoyed to find these pretexts of hope, in order to show that they are concerned and to conceal by the joy which they feign to feel that which they have at seeing the failure of the matter.

183. We run carelessly to the precipice, after we have put something before us to prevent us seeing it.

SECTION IV.

Of the Means of Belief

242. Preface to the second part.—To speak of those who have treated of this matter.

I admire the boldness with which these persons undertake to speak of God. In addressing their argument to infidels, their first chapter is to prove Divinity from the works of nature. I should not be astonished at their enterprise, if they were addressing their argument to the faithful; for it is certain that those who have the living faith in their hearts see at once that all existence is none other than the work of the God whom they adore. But for those in whom this light is extinguished, and in whom we purpose to rekindle it, persons destitute of faith and grace, who, seeking with all their light whatever they see in nature that can bring them to this knowledge, find only obscurity and darkness; to tell them that they have only to look at the smallest things which surround them, and they will see God openly, to give them, as a complete proof of this great and important matter, the course of the moon and planets, and to claim to have concluded the proof with such an argument, is to give them ground for believing that the proofs of our religion are very weak. And I see by reason and experience that nothing is more calculated to arouse their contempt.

It is not after this manner that Scripture speaks, which has a better knowledge of the things that are of God. It says, on the contrary, that God is a hidden God, and that, since the corruption of nature, He has left men in a darkness from which they can escape only through Jesus Christ, without whom all communion with God is cut off. *Nemo novit Patrem, nisi Filius, et cui voluerit Filius revelare.*[30]

This is what Scripture points out to us, when it says in so many places that those who seek God find Him. It is not of that light, "like the noonday sun," that this is said. We do not say that those who seek the noonday sun, or water in the sea, shall find them; and hence the evidence of God must not be of this nature. So it tells us elsewhere: *Vere tu es Deus absconditus.*[31]

243. It is an astounding fact that no canonical writer has ever made use of nature to prove God. They all strive to make us believe in Him. David, Solomon, etc., have never said, "There is no void, therefore there is a God." They must have had more knowledge than the most learned people who came after them, and who have all made use of this argument. This is worthy of attention.

244. "Why! Do you not say yourself that the heavens and birds prove God?" No. "And does your religion not say so"? No. For although it is true in a sense for some souls to whom God gives this light, yet it is false with respect to the majority of men.

245. There are three sources of belief: reason, custom, inspiration. The Christian religion, which alone has reason, does not acknowledge as her true children those who believe without inspiration. It is not that she excludes reason and custom. On the contrary, the mind must be opened to proofs, must be confirmed by custom and offer itself in humbleness to inspirations, which alone can produce a true and saving effect. *Ne evacuetur crux Christi.*[32]

246. Order.—After the letter That we ought to seek God, to write the letter On removing obstacles, which is the discourse on "the machine," on preparing the machine, on seeking by reason.

247. Order.—A letter of exhortation to a friend to induce him to seek. And he will reply, "But what is the use of seeking? Nothing is seen." Then to reply to him, "Do not despair." And he will answer that he would be glad to find some light, but that, according to this very religion, if he believed in it, it will be of no use to him, and that therefore he prefers not to seek. And to answer to that: The machine.

248. A letter which indicates the use of proofs by the machine.—Faith is different from proof; the one is human, the other is a gift of God. *Justus ex fide vivit.*[33] It is this faith that God Himself puts into the heart, of which the proof is often the instrument, *fides ex auditu;*[34] but this faith is in the heart, and makes us not say *scio*, but *credo*.[35]

249. It is superstition to put one's hope in formalities; but it is pride to be unwilling to submit to them.

250. The external must be joined to the internal to obtain anything from God, that is to say, we must kneel, pray with the lips, etc., in order that proud man, who would not submit himself to God, may be now subject to the creature. To expect help from these externals is superstition; to refuse to join them to the internal is pride.

251. Other religions, as the pagan, are more popular, for they consist in externals. But they are not for educated people. A purely intellectual religion would be more suited to the learned, but it would be of no use to the common people. The Christian religion alone is adapted to all, being composed of externals and internals. It raises the common people to the internal, and humbles the proud to the external; it is not perfect without the two, for the people must understand the spirit of the letter,

and the learned must submit their spirit to the letter.

252. For we must not misunderstand ourselves; we are as much automatic as intellectual; and hence it comes that the instrument by which conviction is attained is not demonstrated alone. How few things are demonstrated! Proofs only convince the mind. Custom is the source of our strongest and most believed proofs. It bends the automaton, which persuades the mind without its thinking about the matter. Who has demonstrated that there will be a to-morrow and that we shall die? And what is more believed? It is, then, custom which persuades us of it; it is custom that makes so many men Christians; custom that makes them Turks, heathens, artisans, soldiers, etc. (Faith in baptism is more received among Christians than among Turks.) Finally, we must have recourse to it when once the mind has seen where the truth is, in order to quench our thirst, and steep ourselves in that belief, which escapes us at every hour; for always to have proofs ready is too much trouble. We must get an easier belief, which is that of custom, which, without violence, without art, without argument, makes us believe things and inclines all our powers to this belief, so that our soul falls naturally into it. It is not enough to believe only by force of conviction, when the automaton is inclined to believe the contrary. Both our parts must be made to believe, the mind by reasons which it is sufficient to have seen once in a lifetime,

and the automaton by custom, and by not allowing it to incline to the contrary. *Inclina cor meum, Deus.*[36]

The reason acts slowly, with so many examinations and on so many principles, which must be always present, that at every hour it falls asleep, or wanders, through want of having all its principles present. Feeling does not act thus; it acts in a moment, and is always ready to act. We must then put our faith in feeling; otherwise it will be always vacillating.

253. Two extremes: to exclude reason, to admit reason only.

254. It is not a rare thing to have to reprove the world for too much docility. It is a natural vice like credulity, and as pernicious. Superstition.

255. Piety is different from superstition.

To carry piety as far as superstition is to destroy it.

The heretics reproach us for this superstitious submission. This is to do what they reproach us for...

Infidelity, not to believe in the Eucharist, because it is not seen.

Superstition to believe propositions. Faith, etc.

256. I say there are few true Christians, even as regards faith. There are many who believe but from superstition. There are many who do not believe solely from wickedness. Few are between the two.

In this I do not include those who are of truly pious character, nor all those who believe from a feeling in their heart.

257. There are only three kinds of persons; those who serve God, having found Him; others who are occupied in seeking Him, not having found Him; while the remainder live without seeking Him and without having found Him. The first are reasonable and happy, the last are foolish and unhappy; those between are unhappy and reasonable.

258. *Unusquisque sibi Deum fingit.*[37] Disgust.

259. Ordinary people have the power of not thinking of that about which they do not wish to think. "Do not meditate on the passages about the Messiah, said the Jew to his son. Thus our people often act. Thus are false religions preserved, and even the true one, in regard to many persons.

But there are some who have not the power of thus preventing thought, and who think so much the more as they are forbidden. These undo false religions and even the true one, if they do not find solid arguments.

260. They hide themselves in the press and call numbers to their rescue. Tumult.

Authority.—So far from making it a rule to believe a thing because you have heard it, you ought to believe nothing without putting yourself into the position as if you had never heard it.

It is your own assent to yourself, and the constant voice of your own reason, and not of others, that should make you believe.

Belief is so important! A hundred contradictions might be true. If antiquity were the rule of belief, men of ancient time would then be without rule. If general consent, if men had perished?

False humanity, pride.

Lift the curtain. You try in vain; if you must either believe, or deny, or doubt. Shall we then have no rule? We judge that animals do well what they do. Is there no rule whereby to judge men?

To deny, to believe, and to doubt well, are to a man what the race is to a horse.

Punishment of those who sin, error.

261. Those who do not love the truth take as a pretext that it is disputed, and that a multitude deny it. And so their error arises only from this, that they do not love either truth or charity. Thus they are without excuse.

262. Superstition and lust. Scruples, evil desires. Evil fear; fear, not such as comes from a belief in God, but such as comes from a doubt whether He exists or not. True fear comes from faith; false fear comes from doubt. True fear is joined to hope, because it is born of faith, and because men hope in the God in whom they believe. False fear is joined to despair, because men fear the God in whom they have no belief. The former fear to lose Him; the latter fear to find Him.

263. "A miracle," says one, "would strengthen my faith." He says so when he does not see one. Reasons, seen from afar, appear to limit our view; but when they are reached, we begin to see beyond. Nothing stops the nimbleness of our mind. There is no rule, say we, which has not some exceptions, no truth so general which has not some aspect in which it fails. It is sufficient that it be not absolutely universal to give us a pretext for applying

the exceptions to the present subject and for saying, "This is not always true; there are therefore cases where it is not so." It only remains to show that this is one of them; and that is why we are very awkward or unlucky, if we do not find one some day.

264. We do not weary of eating and sleeping every day, for hunger and sleepiness recur. Without that we should weary of them. So, without the hunger for spiritual things, we weary of them. Hunger after righteousness, the eighth beautitude.

265. Faith indeed tells what the senses do not tell, but not the contrary of what they see. It is above them and not contrary to them.

266. How many stars have telescopes revealed to us which did not exist for our philosophers of old! We freely attack Holy Scripture on the great number of stars, saying, "There are only one thousand and twenty-eight, we know it." There is grass on the earth, we see it—from the moon we would not see it—and on the grass are leaves, and in these leaves are small animals; but after that no more. O presumptuous man! The compounds are composed of elements, and the elements not. O presumptuous man! Here is a fine reflection. We must not say that there is anything which we do not see. We must then talk like others, but not think like them.

267. The last proceeding of reason is to recognise that there is an infinity of things which are beyond it. It is but feeble if it does not see so far as to know this. But if natural things are beyond it, what will be said of supernatural?

268. Submission.—We must know where to doubt, where to feel certain, where to submit. He who does not do so understands not the force of reason. There are some who offend against these three rules, either by affirming everything as demonstrative, from want of knowing what demonstration is; or by doubting everything, from want of knowing where to submit; or by submitting in everything, from want of knowing where they must judge.

269. Submission is the use of reason in which consists true Christianity.

270. Saint Augustine.—Reason would never submit, if it did not judge that there are some occasions on which it ought to submit. It is then right for it to submit, when it judges that it ought to submit.

271. Wisdom sends us to childhood. *Nisi efficiamini sicut parvuli.*[38]

272. There is nothing so conformable to reason as this disavowal of reason.

273. If we submit everything to reason, our religion will have no mysterious and supernatural element. If we offend the principles of reason, our religion will be absurd and ridiculous.

274. All our reasoning reduces itself to yielding to feeling.

But fancy is like, though contrary to, feeling, so that we cannot distinguish between these contraries. One person says that my feeling is fancy, another that his fancy is feeling. We should have a rule. Reason offers itself; but it is pliable in every sense; and thus there is no rule.

275. Men often take their imagination for their heart; and they believe they are converted as soon as they think of being converted.

276. M. de Roannez said: "Reasons come to me afterwards, but at first a thing pleases or shocks me without my knowing the reason, and yet it shocks me for that reason which I only discover afterwards." But I believe, not that it shocked him for the reasons which were found afterwards, but that these reasons were only found because it shocked him.

277. The heart has its reasons, which reason does not know. We feel it in a thousand things. I say that the

heart naturally loves the Universal Being, and also itself naturally, according as it gives itself to them; and it hardens itself against one or the other at its will. You have rejected the one and kept the other. Is it by reason that you love yourself?

278. It is the heart which experiences God, and not the reason. This, then, is faith: God felt by the heart, not by the reason.

Faith is a gift of God; do not believe that we said it was a gift of reasoning. Other religions do not say this of their faith. They only give reasoning in order to arrive at it, and yet it does not bring them to it.

279. Faith is a gift of God; do not believe that we said it was a gift of reasoning. Other religions do not say this of their faith. They only gave reasoning in order to arrive at it, and yet it does not bring them to it.

280. The knowledge of God is very far from the love of Him.

281. Heart, instinct, principles.

282. We know truth, not only by the reason, but also by the heart, and it is in this last way that we know first principles; and reason, which has no part in it, tries in

vain to impugn them. The sceptics, who have only this
for their object, labour to no purpose. We know that
we do not dream, and, however impossible it is for us
to prove it by reason, this inability demonstrates only
the weakness of our reason, but not, as they affirm, the
uncertainty of all our knowledge. For the knowledge
of first principles, as space, time, motion, number, is
as sure as any of those which we get from reasoning.
And reason must trust these intuitions of the heart, and
must base them on every argument. (We have intuitive
knowledge of the tri-dimensional nature of space and of
the infinity of number, and reason then shows that there
are no two square numbers one of which is double of the
other. Principles are intuited, propositions are inferred,
all with certainty, though in different ways.) And it is as
useless and absurd for reason to demand from the heart
proofs of her first principles, before admitting them,
as it would be for the heart to demand from reason
an intuition of all demonstrated propositions before
accepting them.

This inability ought, then, to serve only to humble
reason, which would judge all, but not to impugn our
certainty, as if only reason were capable of instructing
us. Would to God, on the contrary, that we had never
need of it, and that we knew everything by instinct and
intuition! But nature has refused us this boon. On the
contrary, she has given us but very little knowledge

of this kind; and all the rest can be acquired only by reasoning.

Therefore, those to whom God has imparted religion by intuition are very fortunate and justly convinced. But to those who do not have it, we can give it only by reasoning, waiting for God to give them spiritual insight, without which faith is only human and useless for salvation.

283. Order.—Against the objection that Scripture has no order.

The heart has its own order; the intellect has its own, which is by principle and demonstration. The heart has another. We do not prove that we ought to be loved by enumerating in order the causes of love; that would be ridiculous.

Jesus Christ and Saint Paul employ the rule of love, not of intellect; for they would warm, not instruct. It is the same with Saint Augustine. This order consists chiefly in digressions on each point to indicate the end, and keep it always in sight.

284. Do not wonder to see simple people believe without reasoning. God imparts to them love of Him and hatred of self. He inclines their heart to believe.

Men will never believe with a saving and real faith, unless God inclines their heart; and they will believe as soon as He inclines it. And this is what David knew well, when he said: *Inclina cor meum, Deus, in...*[39]

285. Religion is suited to all kinds of minds. Some pay attention only to its establishment, and this religion is such that its very establishment suffices to prove its truth. Others trace it even to the apostles. The more learned go back to the beginning of the world. The angels see it better still, and from a more distant time.

286. Those who believe without having read the Testaments, do so because they have an inward disposition entirely holy, and all that they hear of our religion conforms to it. They feel that a God has made them; they desire only to love God; they desire to hate themselves only. They feel that they have no strength in themselves; that they are incapable of coming to God; and that if God does not come to them, they can have no communion with Him. And they hear our religion say that men must love God only, and hate self only; but that, all being corrupt and unworthy of God, God made Himself man to unite Himself to us. No more is required to persuade men who have this disposition in their heart, and who have this knowledge of their duty and of their inefficiency.

287. Those whom we see to be Christians without the knowledge of the prophets and evidences, nevertheless judge of their religion as well as those who have that knowledge. They judge of it by the heart, as others judge of it by the intellect. God himself inclines them to believe, and thus they are most effectively convinced.

I confess indeed that one of those Christians who believe without proofs will not, perhaps, be capable of convincing an infidel who will say the same of himself. But those who know the proofs of religion will prove without difficulty that such a believer is truly inspired by God, though he cannot prove it himself.

For God having said in His prophecies (which are undoubtedly prophecies) that in the reign of Jesus Christ He would spread His spirit abroad among nations, and that the youths and maidens and children of the Church would prophesy; it is certain that the Spirit of God is in these and not in the others.

288. Instead of complaining that God had hidden Himself, you will give Him thanks for not having revealed so much of Himself; and you will also give Him thanks for not having revealed Himself to haughty sages, unworthy to know so holy a God.

Two kinds of persons know Him: those who have a

humble heart, and who love lowliness, whatever kind of intellect they may have, high or low; and those who have sufficient understanding to see the truth, whatever opposition they may have to it.

289. Proof.—1. The Christian religion, by its establishment, having established itself so strongly, so gently, whilst so contrary to nature. 2. The sanctity, the dignity, and the humility of a Christian soul. 3. The miracles of Holy Scripture. 4. Jesus Christ in particular. 5. The apostles in particular. 6. Moses and the prophets in particular. 7. The Jewish people. 8. The prophecies. 9. Perpetuity; no religion has perpetuity. 10. The doctrine which gives a reason for everything. 11. The sanctity of this law. 12. By the course of the world.

Surely, after considering what is life and what is religion, we should not refuse to obey the inclination to follow it, if it comes into our heart; and it is certain that there is no ground for laughing at those who follow it.

290. Proofs of religion.—Morality, doctrine, miracles, prophecies, types.

SECTION V.

Justice and the Reason of Effects

291. In the letter On Injustice can come the ridiculousness of the law that the elder gets all. "My friend, you were born on this side of the mountain, it is therefore just that your elder brother gets everything."

"Why do you kill me"?

292. He lives on the other side of the water.

293. "Why do you kill me? What! do you not live on the other side of the water? If you lived on this side, my friend, I should be an assassin, and it would be unjust to slay you in this manner. But since you live on the other side, I am a hero, and it is just."

294. On what shall man found the order of the world which he would govern? Shall it be on the caprice of each individual? What confusion! Shall it be on justice? Man is ignorant of it.

Certainly, had he known it, he would not have

established this maxim, the most general of all that obtain among men, that each should follow the custom of his own country. The glory of true equity would have brought all nations under subjection, and legislators would not have taken as their model the fancies and caprice of Persians and Germans instead of this unchanging justice. We would have seen it set up in all the States on earth and in all times; whereas we see neither justice nor injustice which does not change its nature with change in climate. Three degrees of latitude reverse all jurisprudence; a meridian decides the truth. Fundamental laws change after a few years of possession; right has its epochs; the entry of Saturn into the Lion marks to us the origin of such and such a crime. A strange justice that is bounded by a river! Truth on this side of the Pyrenees, error on the other side.

Men admit that justice does not consist in these customs, but that it resides in natural laws, common to every country. They would certainly maintain it obstinately, if reckless chance which has distributed human laws had encountered even one which was universal; but the farce is that the caprice of men has so many vagaries that there is no such law.

Theft, incest, infanticide, parricide, have all had a place among virtuous actions. Can anything be more ridiculous than that a man should have the right to kill me because he lives on the other side of the water, and because his ruler has a quarrel with mine, though I have none with him?

Doubtless there are natural laws; but good reason once corrupted has corrupted all. *Nihil amplius nostrum est; quod nostrum dicimus, artis est.*[40] *Ex senatus—consultis et plebiscitis crimina exercentur.*[41] *Ut olim vitiis, sic nunc legibus laboramus.*[42]

The result of this confusion is that one affirms the essence of justice to be the authority of the legislator; another, the interest of the sovereign; another, present custom, and this is the most sure. Nothing, according to reason alone, is just itself; all changes with time. Custom creates the whole of equity, for the simple reason that it is accepted. It is the mystical foundation of its authority; whoever carries it back to first principles destroys it. Nothing is so faulty as those laws which correct faults. He who obeys them because they are just obeys a justice which is imaginary and not the essence of law; it is quite self-contained, it is law and nothing more. He who will examine its motive will find it so feeble and so trifling that, if he be not accustomed to contemplate the wonders of human imagination, he will marvel that one century has gained for it so much pomp and reverence. The art of opposition and of revolution is to unsettle established customs, sounding them even to their source, to point out their want of authority and justice. We must, it is said, get back to the natural and fundamental laws of the State, which an unjust custom has abolished. It is a game certain to result in the loss of all; nothing will be just on the balance. Yet people readily lend their ear to such arguments. They shake off the yoke as soon as they recognise it; and the great profit by their ruin and by that of these curious investigators of accepted customs. But from a contrary mistake men sometimes think they can justly do everything which is not without an example. That is why the wisest of legislators said that it was necessary to deceive men for their own good; and another, a good politician, *Cum veritatem qua liberetur ignoret, expedit quod fallatur.*[43] We must not see the fact of usurpation; law was once introduced without reason, and has become reasonable. We must make it regarded as authoritative, eternal, and conceal its origin, if we do not wish that it should soon come to an end.

295. Mine, thine.—"This dog is mine," said those poor children; "that is my place in the sun." Here is the beginning and the image of the usurpation of all the earth.

296. When the question for consideration is whether we ought to make war and kill so many men—condemn so many Spaniards to death—only one man is judge, and he is an interested party. There should be a third, who is disinterested.

297. *Veri juris.*[44]—We have it no more; if we had it, we should take conformity to the customs of a country as the rule of justice. It is here that, not finding justice, we have found force, etc.

298. Justice, might.—It is right that what is just should be obeyed; it is necessary that what is strongest should be obeyed. Justice without might is helpless; might without justice is tyrannical. Justice without might is gainsaid, because there are always offenders; might without justice is condemned. We must then combine justice and might and, for this end, make what is just strong, or what is strong just.

Justice is subject to dispute; might is easily recognised and is not disputed. So we cannot give might to justice, because might has gainsaid justice and has declared that it is she herself who is just. And thus, being unable to make what is just strong, we have made what is strong just.

299. The only universal rules are the laws of the country in ordinary affairs and of the majority in others. Whence comes this? From the might which is in them. Hence it comes that kings, who have power of a different kind, do not follow the majority of their ministers.

No doubt equality of goods is just; but, being unable

to cause might to obey justice, men have made it just to obey might. Unable to strengthen justice, they have justified might; so that the just and the strong should unite, and there should be peace, which is the sovereign good.

300. "When a strong man armed keepeth his goods, his goods are in peace."

301. Why do we follow the majority? Is it because they have more reason? No, because they have more power.

Why do we follow the ancient laws and opinions? Is it because they are more sound? No, but because they are unique and remove from us the root of difference.

302. It is the effect of might, not of custom. For those who are capable of originality are few; the greater number will only follow and refuse glory to those inventors who seek it by their inventions. And if these are obstinate in their wish to obtain glory and despise those who do not invent, the latter will call them ridiculous names and will beat them with a stick. Let no one, then, boast of his subtlety, or let him keep his complacency to himself.

303. Might is the sovereign of the world, and not opinion. But opinion makes use of might. It is might

that makes opinion. Gentleness is beautiful in our opinion. Why? Because he who will dance on a rope will be alone, and I win gather a stronger mob of people who will say that it is unbecoming.

304. The cords which bind the respect of men to each other are in general cords of necessity; for there must be different degrees, all men wishing to rule, and not all being able to do so, but some being able.

Let us, then, imagine we see society in the process of formation. Men will doubtless fight till the stronger party overcomes the weaker, and a dominant party is established. But when this is once determined, the masters, who do not desire the continuation of strife, then decree that the power which is in their hands shall be transmitted as they please. Some place it in election by the people, others in hereditary succession, etc.

And this is the point where imagination begins to play its part. Till now power makes fact; now power is sustained by imagination in a certain party, in France in the nobility, in Switzerland in the burgesses, etc.

These cords which bind the respect of men to such and such an individual are therefore the cords of imagination.

305. The Swiss are offended by being called gentlemen, and prove themselves true plebeians in order to be thought worthy of great office.

306. As duchies, kingships, and magistracies are real and necessary, because might rules all, they exist everywhere and always. But since only caprice makes such and such a one a ruler, the principle is not constant, but subject to variation, etc.

307. The chancellor is grave and clothed with ornaments, for his position is unreal. Not so the king; he has power and has nothing to do with the imagination. Judges, physicians, etc., appeal only to the imagination.

308. The habit of seeing kings accompanied by guards, drums, officers, and all the paraphernalia which mechanically inspire respect and awe, makes their countenance, when sometimes seen alone without these accompaniments, impress respect and awe on their subjects; because we cannot separate in thought their persons from the surroundings with which we see them usually joined. And the world, which knows not that this effect is the result of habit, believes that it arises by a natural force, whence come these words, "The character of Divinity is stamped on his countenance," etc.

309. Justice.—As custom determines what is agreeable,

so also does it determine justice.

310. King and tyrant.—I, too, will keep my thoughts secret.

I will take care on every journey.

Greatness of establishment, respect for establishment.

The pleasure of the great is the power to make people happy.

The property of riches is to be given liberally.

The property of each thing must be sought. The property of power is to protect.

When force attacks humbug, when a private soldier takes the square cap off a first president, and throws it out of the window.

311. The government founded on opinion and imagination reigns for some time, and this government is pleasant and voluntary; that founded on might lasts for ever. Thus opinion is the queen of the world, but might is its tyrant.

312. Justice is what is established; and thus all our

established laws will necessarily be regarded as just without examination, since they are established.

313. Sound opinions of the people.—Civil wars are the greatest of evils. They are inevitable, if we wish to reward desert; for all will say they are deserving. The evil we have to fear from a fool who succeeds by right of birth, is neither so great nor so sure.

314. God has created all for Himself. He has bestowed upon Himself the power of pain and pleasure.

You can apply it to God, or to yourself. If to God, the Gospel is the rule. If to yourself, you will take the place of God. As God is surrounded by persons full of charity, who ask of Him the blessings of charity that are in His power, so... recognise, then, and learn that you are only a king of lust, and take the ways of lust.

315. The reason of effects.—It is wonderful that men would not have me honour a man clothed in brocade and followed by seven or eight lackeys! Why! He will have me thrashed, if I do not salute him. This custom is a farce. It is the same with a horse in fine trappings in comparison with another! Montaigne is a fool not to see what difference there is, to wonder at our finding any, and to ask the reason. "Indeed," says he, "how comes it," etc...

316. Sound opinions of the people.—To be spruce is not altogether foolish, for it proves that a great number of people work for one. It shows by one's hair, that one has a valet, a perfumer, etc., by one's band, thread, lace,... etc. Now it is not merely superficial nor merely outward show to have many arms at command. The more arms one has, the more powerful one is. To be spruce is to show one's power.

317. Deference means, "Put yourself to inconvenience." This is apparently silly, but is quite right. For it is to say, "I would indeed put myself to inconvenience if you required it, since indeed I do so when it is of no service to you." Deference further serves to distinguish the great. Now if deference was displayed by sitting in an arm-chair, we should show deference to everybody, and so no distinction would be made; but, being put to inconvenience, we distinguish very well.

318. He has four lackeys.

319. How rightly do we distinguish men by external appearances rather than by internal qualities! Which of us two shall have precedence? Who will give place to the other? The least clever. But I am as clever as he. We should have to fight over this. He has four lackeys, and I have only one. This can be seen; we have only to count. It falls to me to yield, and I am a fool if I contest

the matter. By this means we are at peace, which is the greatest of boons.

320. The most unreasonable things in the world become most reasonable, because of the unruliness of men. What is less reasonable than to choose the eldest son of a queen to rule a State? We do not choose as captain of a ship the passenger who is of the best family.

This law would be absurd and unjust; but, because men are so themselves and always will be so, it becomes reasonable and just. For whom will men choose, as the most virtuous and able? We at once come to blows, as each claims to be the most virtuous and able. Let us then attach this quality to something indisputable. This is the king's eldest son. That is clear, and there is no dispute. Reason can do no better, for civil war is the greatest of evils.

321. Children are astonished to see their comrades respected.

322. To be of noble birth is a great advantage. In eighteen years it places a man within the select circle, known and respected, as another have merited in fifty years. It is a gain of thirty years without trouble.

323. What is the Ego?

Suppose a man puts himself at a window to see those who pass by. If I pass by, can I say that he placed himself there to see me? No; for he does not think of me in particular. But does he who loves someone on account of beauty really love that person? No; for the small-pox, which will kill beauty without killing the person, will cause him to love her no more.

And if one loves me for my judgement, memory, he does not love me, for I can lose these qualities without losing myself. Where, then, is this Ego, if it be neither in the body nor in the soul? And how love the body or the soul, except for these qualities which do not constitute me, since they are perishable? For it is impossible and would be unjust to love the soul of a person in the abstract and whatever qualities might be therein. We never, then, love a person, but only qualities.

Let us, then, jeer no more at those who are honoured on account of rank and office; for we love a person only on account of borrowed qualities.

324. The people have very sound opinions, for example:

> 1. In having preferred diversion and hunting to poetry. The half-learned laugh at it, and glory in being above the folly of the world; but the

people are right for a reason which these do not fathom.

2. In having distinguished men by external marks, as birth or wealth. The world again exults in showing how unreasonable this is; but it is very reasonable. Savages laugh at an infant king.

3. In being offended at a blow, or in desiring glory so much. But it is very desirable on account of the other essential goods which are joined to it; and a man who has received a blow, without resenting it, is overwhelmed with taunts and indignities.

4. In working for the uncertain; in sailing on the sea; in walking over a plank.

325. Montaigne is wrong. Custom should be followed only because it is custom, and not because it is reasonable or just. But people follow it for this sole reason, that they think it just. Otherwise they would follow it no longer, although it were the custom; for they will only submit to reason or justice. Custom without this would pass for tyranny; but the sovereignty of reason and justice is no more tyrannical than that of desire. They are principles natural to man.

It would, therefore, be right to obey laws and customs, because they are laws; but we should know that there is neither truth nor justice to introduce into them, that we know nothing of these, and so must follow what is accepted. By this means we would never depart from them. But people cannot accept this doctrine; and, as they believe that truth can be found, and that it exists in law and custom, they believe them and take their antiquity as a proof of their truth, and not simply of their authority apart from truth. Thus they obey laws, but they are liable to revolt when these are proved to be valueless; and this can be shown of all, looked at from a certain aspect.

326. Injustice.——It is dangerous to tell the people that the laws are unjust; for they obey them only because they think them just. Therefore it is necessary to tell them at the same time that they must obey them because they are laws, just as they must obey superiors, not because they are just, but because they are superiors. In this way all sedition is prevented, if this can be made intelligible and it be understood what is the proper definition of justice.

327. The world is a good judge of things, for it is in natural ignorance, which is man's true state. The sciences have two extremes which meet. The first is the pure natural ignorance in which all men find themselves at birth.

The other extreme is that reached by great intellects, who, having run through all that men can know, find they know nothing, and come back again to that same ignorance from which they set out; but this is a learned ignorance which is conscious of itself. Those between the two, who have departed from natural ignorance and not been able to reach the other, have some smattering of this vain knowledge and pretend to be wise. These trouble the world and are bad judges of everything. The people and the wise constitute the world; these despise it, and are despised. They judge badly of everything, and the world judges rightly of them.

328. The reason of effects.—Continual alternation of pro and con.

We have, then, shown that man is foolish, by the estimation he makes of things which are not essential; and all these opinions are destroyed. We have next shown that all these opinions are very sound and that thus, since all these vanities are well founded, the people are not so foolish as is said. And so we have destroyed the opinion which destroyed that of the people.

But we must now destroy this last proposition and show that it remains always true that the people are foolish, though their opinions are sound because they do not perceive the truth where it is, and, as they place it where it is not, their opinions are always very false and very unsound.

329. The reason of effects.—The weakness of man is the reason why so many things are considered fine, as to be good at playing the lute. It is only an evil because of our weakness.

330. The power of kings is founded on the reason and on the folly of the people, and specially on their folly. The greatest and most important thing in the world has weakness for its foundation, and this foundation is wonderfully sure; for there is nothing more sure than this, that the people will be weak. What is based on sound reason is very ill-founded as the estimate of wisdom.

331. We can only think of Plato and Aristotle in grand academic robes. They were honest men, like others, laughing with their friends, and, when they diverted themselves with writing their Laws and the Politics, they did it as an amusement. That part of their life was the least philosophic and the least serious; the most philosophic was to live simply and quietly. If they wrote on politics, it was as if laying down rules for a lunatic asylum; and if they presented the appearance of speaking of a great matter, it was because they knew that the madmen, to whom they spoke, thought they were kings and

emperors. They entered into their principles in order to make their madness as little harmful as possible.

332. Tyranny consists in the desire of universal power beyond its scope.

There are different assemblies of the strong, the fair, the sensible, the pious, in which each man rules at home, not elsewhere. And sometimes they meet, and the strong and the fair foolishly fight as to who shall be master, for their mastery is of different kinds. They do not understand one another, and their fault is the desire to rule everywhere. Nothing can effect this, not even might, which is of no use in the kingdom of the wise, and is only mistress of external actions.

Tyranny—So these expressions are false and tyrannical: "I am fair, therefore I must be feared. I am strong, therefore I must be loved. I am...

Tyranny is the wish to have in one way what can only be had in another. We render different duties to different merits; the duty of love to the pleasant; the duty of fear to the strong; duty of belief to the learned.

We must render these duties; it is unjust to refuse them, and unjust to ask others. And so it is false and tyrannical to say, "He is not strong, therefore I will not esteem him; he is not able, therefore I will not fear him."

333. Have you never seen people who, in order to complain of the little fuss you make about them, parade before you the example of great men who esteem them? In answer I reply to them, "Show me the merit whereby you have charmed these persons, and I also will esteem you."

334. The reason of effects.—Lust and force are the source of all our actions; lust causes voluntary actions, force involuntary ones.

335. The reason of effects.—It is, then, true to say that all the world is under a delusion; for, although the opinions of the people are sound, they are not so as conceived by them, since they think the truth to be where it is not. Truth is indeed in their opinions, but not at the point where they imagine it. Thus it is true that we must honour noblemen, but not because noble birth is real superiority, etc.

336. The reason of effects.—We must keep our thought secret, and judge everything by it, while talking like the people.

337. The reason of effects. Degrees. The people honour persons of high birth. The semi-learned despise

them, saying that birth is not a personal, but a chance superiority. The learned honour them, not for popular reasons, but for secret reasons. Devout persons, who have more zeal than knowledge, despise them, in spite of that consideration which makes them honoured by the learned, because they judge them by a new light which piety gives them. But perfect Christians honour them by another and higher light. So arise a succession of opinions for and against, according to the light one has.

338. True Christians, nevertheless, comply with folly, not because they respect folly, but the command of God, who for the punishment of men has made them subject to these follies. *Omnis creatura subjecta est vanitati.*[45] *Liberabitur.*[46] Thus Saint Thomas explains the passage in Saint James on giving place to the rich, that, if they do it not in the sight of God, they depart from the command of religion.

SECTION VIII.

The Fundamentals of the Christian Religion

556. Men blaspheme what they do not know. The Christian religion consists in two points. It is of equal concern to men to know them, and it is equally dangerous to be ignorant of them. And it is equally of God's mercy that He has given indications of both.

And yet they take occasion to conclude that one of these points does not exist, from that which should have caused them to infer the other. The sages who have said there is only one God have been persecuted, the Jews were hated, and still more the Christians. They have seen by the light of nature that if there be a true religion on earth, the course of all things must tend to it as to a centre.

The whole course of things must have for its object the establishment and the greatness of religion. Men must have within them feelings suited to what religion teaches us. And, finally, religion must so be the object and the centre to which all things tend that whoever knows the principles of religion can give an explanation both of the whole nature of man in particular and of the whole course of the world in general.

And on this ground they take occasion to revile the Christian religion, because they misunderstand it. They imagine that it consists simply in the worship of a God considered as great, powerful, and eternal; which is strictly deism, almost as far removed from the Christian religion as atheism, which is its exact opposite. And thence they conclude that this religion is not true, because they do not see that all things concur to the establishment of this point, that God does not manifest Himself to men with all the evidence which He could show.

But let them conclude what they will against deism, they will conclude nothing against the Christian religion, which properly consists in the mystery of the Redeemer, who, uniting in Himself the two natures, human and divine, has redeemed men from the corruption of sin in order to reconcile them in His divine person to God.

The Christian religion, then, teaches men these two truths; that there is a God whom men can know, and that there is a corruption in their nature which renders them unworthy of Him. It is equally important to men to know both these points; and it is equally dangerous for man to know God without knowing his own wretchedness, and to know his own wretchedness without knowing the Redeemer who can free him from it. The knowledge of only one of these points gives rise either to the pride of philosophers, who have known God, and not their own wretchedness, or to the despair of atheists, who know their own wretchedness, but not the Redeemer.

And, as it is alike necessary to man to know these two points, so is it alike merciful of God to have made us know them. The Christian religion does this; it is in this that it consists.

Let us herein examine the order of the world and see if all things do not tend to establish these two chief points of this religion: Jesus Christ is end of all, and the centre to which all tends. Whoever knows Him knows the reason of everything.

Those who fall into error err only through failure to see one of these two things. We can, then, have an excellent knowledge of God without that of our own wretchedness and of our own wretchedness without that of God. But we cannot know Jesus Christ without knowing at the same time both God and our own wretchedness.

Therefore I shall not undertake here to prove by natural

reasons either the existence of God, or the Trinity, or the immortality of the soul, or anything of that nature; not only because I should not feel myself sufficiently able to find in nature arguments to convince hardened atheists, but also because such knowledge without Jesus Christ is useless and barren. Though a man should be convinced that numerical proportions are immaterial truths, eternal and dependent on a first truth, in which they subsist and which is called God, I should not think him far advanced towards his own salvation.

The God of Christians is not a God who is simply the author of mathematical truths, or of the order of the elements; that is the view of heathens and Epicureans. He is not merely a God who exercises His providence over the life and fortunes of men, to bestow on those who worship Him a long and happy life. That was the portion of the Jews. But the God of Abraham, the God of Isaac, the God of Jacob, the God of Christians, is a God of love and of comfort, a God who fills the soul and heart of those whom He possesses, a God who makes them conscious of their inward wretchedness, and His infinite mercy, who unites Himself to their inmost soul, who fills it with humility and joy, with confidence and love, who renders them incapable of any other end than Himself.

All who seek God without Jesus Christ, and who rest

in nature, either find no light to satisfy them, or come to form for themselves a means of knowing God and serving Him without a mediator. Thereby they fall either into atheism, or into deism, two things which the Christian religion abhors almost equally.

Without Jesus Christ the world would not exist; for it should needs be either that it would be destroyed or be a hell.

If the world existed to instruct man of God, His divinity would shine through every part in it in an indisputable manner; but as it exists only by Jesus Christ, and for Jesus Christ, and to teach men both their corruption and their redemption, all displays the proofs of these two truths.

All appearance indicates neither a total exclusion nor a manifest presence of divinity, but the presence of a God who hides himself. Everything bears this character.

Shall he alone who knows his nature know it only to be miserable? Shall he alone who knows it be alone unhappy?

He must not see nothing at all, nor must he see sufficient for him to believe he possesses it; but he must see enough to know that he has lost it. For to know of his loss, he must see and not see; and that is exactly the state in which he naturally is.

Whatever part he takes, I shall not leave him at rest.

557. It is, then, true that everything teaches man his condition, but he must understand this well. For it is not true that all reveals God, and it is not true that all conceals God. But it is at the same time true that He hides Himself from those who tempt Him, and that He reveals Himself to those who seek Him, because men are both unworthy and capable of God; unworthy by their corruption, capable by their original nature.

558. What shall we conclude from all our darkness, but our unworthiness?

559. If there never had been any appearance of God, this eternal deprivation would have been equivocal, and might have as well corresponded with the absence of all divinity, as with the unworthiness of men to know Him; but His occasional, though not continual, appearances remove the ambiguity. If He appeared once, He exists always; and thus we cannot but conclude both that there is a God and that men are unworthy of Him.

560. We do not understand the glorious state of Adam, nor the nature of his sin, nor the transmission of it to us.

These are matters which took place under conditions of a nature altogether different from our own and which transcend our present understanding.

The knowledge of all this is useless to us as a means of escape from it; and all that we are concerned to know is that we are miserable, corrupt, separated from God, but ransomed by Jesus Christ, whereof we have wonderful proofs on earth.

So the two proofs of corruption and redemption are drawn from the ungodly, who live in indifference to religion, and from the Jews who are irreconcilable enemies.

561. There are two ways of proving the truths of our religion; one by the power of reason, the other by the authority of him who speaks.

We do not make use of the latter, but of the former. We do not say, "This must be believed, for Scripture, which says it, is divine." But we say that it must be believed for such and such a reason, which are feeble arguments, as reason may be bent to everything.

562. There is nothing on earth that does not show either the wretchedness of man, or the mercy of God; either the weakness of man without God, or the strength of man with God.

563. It will be one of the confusions of the damned to see that they are condemned by their own reason, by which they claimed to condemn the Christian religion.

564. The prophecies, the very miracles and proofs of our religion, are not of such a nature that they can be said to be absolutely convincing. But they are also of such a kind that it cannot be said that it is unreasonable to believe them. Thus there is both evidence and obscurity to enlighten some and confuse others. But the evidence is such that it surpasses, or at least equals, the evidence to the contrary; so that it is not reason which can determine men not to follow it, and thus it can only be lust or malice of heart. And by this means there is sufficient evidence to condemn, and insufficient to convince; so that it appears in those who follow it that it is grace, and not reason, which makes them follow it; and in those who shun it, that it is lust, not reason, which makes them shun it.

Vere discipuli, vere Israelita, vere liberi, vere cibus.[100]

565. Recognise, then, the truth of religion in the very obscurity of religion, in the little light we have of it, and in the indifference which we have to knowing it.

566. We understand nothing of the works of God, if we do not take as a principle that He has willed to blind some and enlighten others.

567. The two contrary reasons. We must begin with that; without that we understand nothing, and all is heretical; and we must even add at the end of each truth that the opposite truth is to be remembered.

568. Objection. The Scripture is plainly full of matters not dictated by the Holy Spirit. Answer. Then they do not harm faith. Objection. But the Church has decided that all is of the Holy Spirit. Answer. I answer two things: first, the Church has not so decided; secondly, if she should so decide, it could be maintained.

Do you think that the prophecies cited in the Gospel are related to make you believe? No, it is to keep you from believing.

569. Canonical.—The heretical books in the beginning of the Church serve to prove the canonical.

570. To the chapter on the Fundamentals must be added that on Typology touching the reason of types: why Jesus Christ was prophesied as to His first coming; why prophesied obscurely as to the manner.

571. The reason why. Types.—They had to deal with a carnal people and to render them the depositary of the spiritual covenant. To give faith to the Messiah, it was necessary there should have been precedent prophesies,

and that these should be conveyed by persons above suspicion, diligent, faithful, unusually zealous, and known to all the world.

To accomplish all this, God chose this carnal people, to whom He entrusted the prophecies which foretell the Messiah as a deliverer and as a dispenser of those carnal goods which this people loved. And thus they have had an extraordinary passion for their prophets and, in sight of the whole world, have had charge of these books which foretell their Messiah, assuring all nations that He should come and in the way foretold in the books, which they held open to the whole world. Yet this people, deceived by the poor and ignominious advent of the Messiah, have been His most cruel enemies. So that they, the people least open to suspicion in the world of favouring us, the most strict and most zealous that can be named for their law and their prophets, have kept the books incorrupt. Hence those who have rejected and crucified Jesus Christ, who has been to them an offence, are those who have charge of the books which testify of Him, and state that He will be an offence and rejected. Therefore they have shown it was He by rejecting Him, and He has been alike proved both by the righteous Jews who received Him and by the unrighteous who rejected Him, both facts having been foretold.

Wherefore the prophecies have a hidden and spiritual

meaning to which this people were hostile, under the carnal meaning which they loved. If the spiritual meaning had been revealed, they would not have loved it, and, unable to bear it, they would not have been zealous of the preservation of their books and their ceremonies; and if they had loved these spiritual promises, and had preserved them incorrupt till the time of the Messiah, their testimony would have had no force, because they had been his friends.

Therefore it was well that the spiritual meaning should be concealed; but, on the other hand, if this meaning had been so hidden as not to appear at all, it could not have served as a proof of the Messiah. What then was done? In a crowd of passages it has been hidden under the temporal meaning, and in a few been clearly revealed; besides that, the time and the state of the world have been so clearly foretold that it is clearer than the sun. And in some places this spiritual meaning is so clearly expressed that it would require a blindness, like that which the flesh imposes on the spirit when it is subdued by it, not to recognise it.

See, then, what has been the prudence of God. This meaning is concealed under another in an infinite number of passages, and in some, though rarely, it is revealed; but yet so that the passages in which it is concealed are equivocal and can suit both meanings; whereas the passages where it is disclosed are unequivocal and can only suit the spiritual meaning.

So that this cannot lead us into error and could only be misunderstood by so carnal a people.

For when blessings are promised in abundance, what was to prevent them from understanding the true blessings, but their covetousness, which limited the meaning to worldly goods? But those whose only good was in God referred them to God alone. For there are two principles, which divide the wills of men, covetousness and charity. Not that covetousness cannot exist along with faith in God, nor charity with worldly riches; but covetousness uses God and enjoys the world, and charity is the opposite.

Now the ultimate end gives names to things. All which prevents us from attaining it is called an enemy to us. Thus the creatures, however good, are the enemies of the righteous, when they turn them away from God, and God Himself is the enemy of those whose covetousness He confounds.

Thus as the significance of the word enemy is dependent on the ultimate end, the righteous understood by it their passions, and the carnal the Babylonians; and so these terms were obscure only for the unrighteous. And this is what Isaiah says: *Signa legem in electis meis,*[101] and that Jesus Christ shall be a stone of stumbling. But, "Blessed are they who shall not be offended in him." Hosea 14:9, says excellently, "Where is the wise? and he shall understand what I say. The righteous shall know them, for the ways of God are right; but the transgressors shall fall therein."

572. Hypothesis that the apostles were impostors. The time clearly, the manner obscurely. Five typical proofs.

1,600 prophets.
400 scattered.

2,000

573. Blindness of Scripture.—"The Scripture," said the Jews, "says that we shall not know whence Christ will come (John 7:27, and 12:34)—The Scripture says that Christ abideth for ever, and He said that He should die." Therefore, says Saint John, they believed not, though He had done so many miracles, that the word of Isaiah might be fulfilled:"He hath blinded them," etc.

574. Greatness.—Religion is so great a thing that it is right that those who will not take the trouble to seek it, if it be obscure, should be deprived of it. Why, then, do any complain, if it be such as can be found by seeking?

575. All things work together for good to the elect, even the obscurities of Scripture; for they honour them because of what is divinely clear. And all things work together for evil to the rest of the world, even what is clear; for they revile such, because of the obscurities which they do not understand.

576. The general conduct of the world towards the Church: God willing to blind and to enlighten.—The event having proved the divinity of these prophecies, the rest ought to be believed. And thereby we see the order of the world to be of this kind. The miracles of the Creation and the Deluge being forgotten, God sends the law and the miracles of Moses, the prophets who prophesied particular things; and to prepare a lasting miracle, He prepares prophecies and their fulfilment; but, as the prophecies could be suspected, He desires to make them above suspicion, etc.

577. God has made the blindness of this people subservient to the good of the elect.

578. There is sufficient clearness to enlighten the elect, and sufficient obscurity to humble them. There is sufficient obscurity to blind the reprobate, and sufficient clearness to condemn them and make them inexcusable. Saint Augustine, Montaigne, Sebond.

The genealogy of Jesus Christ in the Old Testament is intermingled with so many others that are useless that it cannot be distinguished. If Moses had kept only the record of the ancestors of Christ, that might have been too plain. If he had not noted that of Jesus Christ, it might not have been sufficiently plain. But, after all, whoever looks closely sees that of Jesus Christ expressly traced through Tamar, Ruth, etc.

Those who ordained these sacrifices knew their uselessness; those who have declared their uselessness, have not ceased to practise them.

If God had permitted only one religion, it has been too easily known; but when we look at it closely, we clearly discern the truth amidst this confusion.

The premiss.—Moses was a clever man. If, then, he ruled himself by his reason, he would say nothing clearly which was directly against reason.

Thus all the very apparent weaknesses are strength. Example; the two genealogies in Saint Matthew and Saint Luke. What can be clearer than that this was not concerted?

579. God (and the Apostles), foreseeing that the seeds of pride would make heresies spring up, and being

unwilling to give them occasion to arise from correct expressions, has put in Scripture and the prayers of the Church contrary words and sentences to produce their fruit in time.

So in morals He gives charity, which produces fruits contrary to lust.

580. Nature has some perfections to show that she is the image of God, and some defects to show that she is only His image.

581. God prefers rather to incline the will than the intellect. Perfect clearness would be of use to the intellect and would harm the will. To humble pride.

582. We make an idol of truth itself; for truth apart from charity is not God, but His image and idol, which we must neither love nor worship; and still less must we love or worship its opposite, namely, falsehood.

I can easily love total darkness; but if God keeps me in a state of semi-darkness, such partial darkness displeases me, and, because I do not see therein the advantage of total darkness, it is unpleasant to me. This is a fault and a sign that I make for myself an idol of darkness, apart from the order of God. Now only His order must be worshipped.

583. The feeble-minded are people who know the truth, but only affirm it so far as consistent with their own interest. But, apart from that, they renounce it.

584. The world exists for the exercise of mercy and judgement, not as if men were placed in it out of the hands of God, but as hostile to God; and to them He grants by grace sufficient light, that they may return to Him, if they desire to seek and follow Him; and also that they may be punished, if they refuse to seek or follow Him.

585. That God has willed to hide Himself.—If there were only one religion, God would indeed be manifest. The same would be the case if there were no martyrs but in our religion.

God being thus hidden, every religion which does not affirm that God is hidden is not true; and every religion which does not give the reason of it is not instructive. Our religion does all this: *Vere tu es Deus absconditus.*[102]

586. If there were no obscurity, man would not be sensible of his corruption; if there were no light, man would not hope for a remedy. Thus, it is not only fair, but advantageous to us, that God be partly hidden and partly revealed; since it is equally dangerous to man to know God without knowing his own wretchedness, and

to know his own wretchedness without knowing God.

587. This religion, so great in miracles, saints, blameless Fathers, learned and great witnesses, martyrs, established kings as David, and Isaiah, a prince of the blood, and so great in science, after having displayed all her miracles and all her wisdom, rejects all this, and declares that she has neither wisdom nor signs, but only the cross and foolishness.

For those, who, by these signs and that wisdom, have deserved your belief, and who have proved to you their character, declare to you that nothing of all this can change you, and render you capable of knowing and loving God, but the power of the foolishness of the cross without wisdom and signs, and not the signs without this power. Thus our religion is foolish in respect to the effective cause and wise in respect to the wisdom which prepares it.

588. Our religion is wise and foolish. Wise, because it is the most learned and the most founded on miracles, prophecies, etc. Foolish, because it is not all this which makes us belong to it. This makes us, indeed, condemn those who do not belong to it; but it does not cause belief in those who do belong to it. It is the cross that makes them believe, *ne evacuata sit crux*.[103] And so Saint Paul, who came with wisdom and signs, says that he has

come neither with wisdom nor with signs; for he came to convert. But those who come only to convince can say that they come with wisdom and with signs.

SECTION II.

5. Title given by Pico della Mirandola to one of his proposed nine hundred theses, in 1486.

6. Tacitus, *Annals*, iv. "Kindnesses are agreeable so long as one thinks them possible to render; further, recognition makes way for hatred."

7. St. Augustine, *City of God*, xxi. 10. "The manner in which the spirit is united to the body can not be understood by man; and yet it is man."

8. Virgil, *Georgics*, ii. "Happy is he who is able to know the causes of things."

9. Horace, *Epistles*, I. vi. 1. "To be astonished at nothing is nearly the only thing which can give and conserve happiness."

10. Cicero, *Disputationes Tusculanae*, i, ii *Harum sententiarum quae vera sit, Deus aliquis viderit.* "Which of these opinions in the truth, a god will see."

11. Montaigne, *Essays*, ii.

12. Montaigne, *Essays*, ii.

13. Treatise on the Vacuum.

14. Terence, *Heauton Timorumenos*, III. v. 8. "There is one who will say great foolishness with great effort."

15. Montaigne, *Essays*, ii.

16. Pliny, ii. "As though there were anyone more unhappy than a man dominated by his imagination."

17. Cicero, *De Divinatione* ii. 22. "A common happening does not astonish, even though the cause is unknown; an event such as one has never seen before passes for a prodigy."

18. Allusion to Gen. 7. 14. *Ipsi et omne animal secundus genus suum.* "And every beast after his kind."

19. Homer, *Odyssey*, xviii.
20. Livy, xxxiv. 17. "A brutal people, for whom, when they have not armour, there is not life."
21. Ecclus. 24:11. "With all these I have sought rest."

SECTION IV.

30. Matt. 11:27. "Neither knoweth any man the Father, save the Son, and he to whomsoever the Son will reveal him."
31. Is. 45:15. "Verily, thou art a God that hidest thyself."
32. 1 Cor. 1:17. "Lest the cross of Christ should be made of none effect."
33. Rom. 1:17. "The just shall live by faith."
34. Rom. 10:17. "Faith cometh by hearing."
35. "I know." "I believe."
36. Ps. 119. 36. "Incline my heart, O Lord."
37. Wisd. of Sol. 15:8, 16. "He moulds a God... like unto himself."
38. Matt. 18:3. "Except ye become as little children."
39. Ps. 119:36. "Incline my heart, O Lord, unto thy testimonies."

SECTION V.

40. Cicero, *De finibus*, V. 21. "There is no longer anything which is ours; what I call ours is conventional."
41. Seneca, *Epistles*, xcv. "It is by virtue of senatus-consultes and plebiscites that one commits crimes."
42. Tacitus, *Annals*, iii. 25. "Once we suffered from our vices; today we suffer from our laws."
43. Saint Augustine, *City of God*, iv. 27. "As he has ignored the truth which frees, it is right he is mistaken."
44. Cicero, *De officiis*, iii, 17. "Concerning true law."
45. Eccles. 3:19. "for all is vanity."
46. Rom. 8:20–21. "It shall be delivered."

SECTION VIII.

100. Allusion to John 6:56; 1:47; 8:36; 6:32. "True disciple; an Israelite indeed; free indeed; true bread."

101. *In discipulis meis.* Isaiah 8:16. "Seal the law among my disciples."

102. Is. 45:15.

103. 1 Cor. 1:17. "Lest the cross of Christ should be made of none effect."